The Five Steps of the Self-Reliance Program

SURRENDER
Recognize the temporary superiority
of the situation.

WITHDRAWAL
Embrace your solitude,
and learn to identify
the brain-soul connection.

REEVALUATION
Examine your expectations, beliefs,
and self-esteem.

REEMERGENCE
Establish seven new rules
to take the place of the old ones.

DISCOVERY
Take up the challenge of finding
your own inner truth.

LIVING TOGETHER, FEELING ALONE

Healing Your Hidden Loneliness

Dr. Dan Kiley

FAWCETT CREST • NEW YORK

A Fawcett Crest Book
Published by Ballantine Books
Copyright © 1989 by Dr. Dan Kiley

Library of Congress Catalog Card Number: 89-33433

ISBN 0-449-21919-4

This edition published by arrangement with Prentice Hall Press, a division of Simon and Schuster, Inc.

Manufactured in the United States of America

First Ballantine Books Edition: March 1991

When a behavioral scientist ventures into unknown territory, he or she typically uses case studies to describe both the symptoms of his or her discovery and the treatment used to allay those symptoms. I've tried to follow this course of study yet bring you a text whose ideas and recommendations are easily read and even more easily implemented.

I've studied more than one hundred cases of Living Together Loneliness in the past five years and have encountered hundreds more. The situations you'll read about in this book are entirely true. However, I've camouflaged the identity of the women and remind you that any similarity between a woman described in this book and a woman you may know is purely coincidental and unintended.

Contents

Preface   ix
Acknowledgments   xi

Part I   Background   1
  1   Living Together Loneliness   19
  2   Are You Lonely? / The Stages of LTL   30
  3   External Causes of LTL   49
  4   Internal Causes of LTL   62
  5   Symptoms of LTL   90

Part II   Treatment   123
  6   Step One: Surrender   128
  7   Step Two: Withdrawal   144
  8   Step Three: Reevaluation   165
  9   Step Four: Reemergence   185
 10   Step Five: Discovery   201
    Epilogue   218
    Suggested Readings   221

Preface

It was March of 1969, six months after I'd received my doctorate in psychology. I was sitting in my clinic office listening to a woman complain about how her fourteen-year-old son unmercifully teased his younger sister.

"What am I going to do," she asked pleadingly, "when, at four-fifteen, Josh comes home and starts picking on Tina?"

Still a novice, I launched into a detailed psychological analysis of the adolescent, complete with phrases such as "key moments of self-development" and "normal adolescent rebellion."

"Yes," she sighed patiently, "but what am I going to *do*?"

Giving her the best that my textbooks had to offer, I continued to barrage her with theoretical hypotheses and philosophical overviews.

She had a dejected look on her face. It was clear that I had no answer to the distressed woman's question. And the reason was that she wasn't asking me to solve her problem. Rather, what she wanted and needed were a couple of options for action.

Since then, the major thrust of my work over the past twenty years has been to draw upon research and experience in the area of generating options for problematic situations. I've ceased to worry as I once did that the people with whom I work might blindly follow my recommendations. No matter how prescriptive my advice, or how emotional my appeal for change, people are going to do what they choose to do.

This book has proved to be my most difficult challenge in the area of generating options. In it I describe a complicated phenomenon that has never before been delineated. Loneliness is a unique experience that often touches the center of a person's soul. Any program for overcoming loneliness, especially something as difficult to validate as *Living Together, Feeling Alone*, must allow a person latitude to dig inside herself and discover new perspectives about life.

Two major changes in my clinical work have enabled me to meet this challenge. First, I've been able to listen to many women throughout the world with a wide range of problems. This, together with long-term counseling of hundreds of women in my office, has given me confidence in my option-giving, trouble-shooter role with women.

As a result of this exposure, I've been more successful treating women than men. With men, I lose my objectivity, too easily assuming that I *know* what they're talking about. But with women, I've learned to take nothing for granted, to study more carefully, to consult the research more often, and to listen twice and speak once. The result is that my options for women are based more on proven fact than on my biases.

The second change in my work followed my contact with an unorthodox teacher, a Cherokee Indian medicine man. I happened upon George Bighorn as part of a search for greater meaning in my own life. As I reflected upon the philosophy of Indian medicine (which he called ''the traditional way''), I rediscovered a sense of spirituality, both in myself and in people who asked me for help.

The combination of my long-standing pragmatism and my renewed spirituality gave me a more balanced perspective, one that enabled me to address the subject of loneliness, including both the subjectivity the topic requires and the objectivity that so many women demand.

Please don't mistake my recommendations for the thoughtless outcroppings of the latest trendy, new-age enlightenment. I'm not heralding the traditional way as an emotional panacea. There's much about it that I find unsuitable for the problems facing our society. But it has too much to offer not to let it influence me, especially in confronting the harsh realities of *Living Together, Feeling Alone*.

My spiritual recommendations have a definite prescriptive nature to them. I call this new approach to counseling and advice "Spiritual Behaviorism." If the concept sounds a bit strange to you, please delay judgment until you've sampled the wares.

Acknowledgment

A special thanks goes to Marilyn Abraham, the editor in chief of Prentice Hall Press. She, along with the publisher, Liz Perle, saw the potential in what had become a rather stodgy professional study. Marilyn worked long and hard in helping, and even pushing me at times, to find the diamond that existed among the lumps of coal.

An author does not live by his skill alone, at least not this author. Howard Morhaim is a literary agent's literary agent. He's become so important to my work that I trust his every thought and impulse. He's an honorable and decent man, and I hope the publishing world appreciates him as much as I do.

For those of you who've read my earlier books, it may seem repetitious that I again thank my wife, Nancy, for her invaluable contribution to my work. But it's true, and must be said again. A man who has a good woman is indeed a lucky man. I'm the luckiest.

In showing my appreciation to the women who formed the research group for this project, I would especially like to thank them for reinforcing my belief in this simple guideline: To have never been lonely is to never have loved—and that's too big a price to pay.

PART I

Background

LONELINESS is viewed as a condition affecting shy people with no friends, the recently widowed or divorced, and unhappy singles. Therefore, if a woman is married or living with a man, and if she has a busy schedule, it might not even enter her mind that she's capable of experiencing debilitating loneliness.

However, after considerable study, I've come to the conclusion that there are *two* types of loneliness. One type is the loneliness we're most familiar with—a type I call "uncoupled" loneliness. The other is the loneliness that affects women who are coupled (whether married or living together). I say that they are *Living Together, Feeling Alone*. To distinguish it from other types of lonely feelings, I refer to it as "Living Together Loneliness," abbreviated as LTL.

LTL IS A REAL PROBLEM

It's very difficult for the LTL woman to validate her experiences as legitimate. She doesn't feel that she has a *right* to be lonely. She looks around herself and thinks that she should be happy. If she were to tell a friend about being lonely, it's possible she wouldn't get much support. "You've got Fred," the friend might say, "what are you complaining about?"

It never dawns on her that living with someone and still being lonely is a *real* problem. Because it's so hard to validate, LTL can create more psychological stress than uncoupled loneliness.

It's estimated that more than one-fourth of the population regularly suffers from loneliness. The vast majority of these sufferers are female (males typically are unwilling to acknowledge lonely feelings). If you apply this percentage to the problem of LTL and then consider that there are 50 million marriages and millions of couples living together, it's possible that between *10 and 20 million* women are *Living Together, Feeling Alone*. If men who do experience loneliness are included, this number is much higher.

Many an LTL woman is involved in a dysfunctional relationship but is extremely reluctant to leave. She is besieged with fears of "making it" on her own and suffers with the guilt of somehow having "caused" the troubles in her marriage. Also, she knows that divorce is no miracle cure.

The LTL woman is not mentally ill, nor is she uneducated, undersocialized, mentally deficient, or otherwise psychologically impaired. Quite the contrary, she's often a college-educated, professional woman and mother, who demonstrates her social and personal competence in all areas of her life.

My studies have allowed me to compile two profiles of the LTL woman. The first is a profile of her inner world. It describes the personality traits that set the stage for the LTL experience. The second profile describes symptoms which appear in the acute stage of LTL.

Inner Profile

- Although she tries to hide it, she has low self-esteem.

- Her fears (of rejection, of being alone, of her own anger, or a combination thereof) trap her.

- She is insecure in love due to the lack of unconditional love given her during her childhood.

- She denies emotional pain until it forces itself into her consciousness.

- She takes too much responsibility for the happiness and welfare of other people.

- She often feels powerless, believing that she can't do anything about her emotional pain.

Outer Profile

- The woman is thirty-three to forty-six, married, has a comfortable lifestyle, and may or may not have children. If not working outside the home, she's very busy as a mother and community activist.

- She blames her partner for her loneliness. Often, he's critical, demanding, and uncommunicative.

- Her bitterness has reached a point where she realizes that she's becoming obsessed with it.

- She experiences a hint of estrangement from other people, even her good friends.

- She's having or is thinking about having an affair.

- She's seeking or has sought counseling for depression or anxiety.

- She's nearly obsessed with her weight, often fighting a weight problem unsuccessfully.

- She's in danger of becoming addicted to drugs or alcohol (she may already be).

- She may have a recurring fantasy or thought about her partner dying.

If you saw yourself in the first profile, but not in the second, be thankful. Either your situation is not as serious as it might be, or you still have time to avoid the more devastating consequences of LTL. If you saw a bit of yourself in both profiles, take heart, this book will help you a great deal.

One of my primary goals in this book is to give the LTL woman this validation: *Your loneliness is a real problem, and if you accept it without shame and learn from it without blame, you'll become an even better person for having dealt with it.*

THE DEATH FANTASY

I was giving a speech to several hundred women in a midwestern city, talking about men who resist change. I said that many men were overwhelmed by insecurity but covered it with a macho attitude. I spoke personally, including myself as one of an increasing number of men who realize that they must guard against excessive self-involvement.

I ended my emotional appeal by announcing the startling results of a recent research project. "Men who are excessively self-involved," I said emphatically, "are six times more likely to die of coronary heart disease than men who are not."

I let the silence punctuate my message. And then, within a second or two, from somewhere on the right side of the audience, a woman yelled, "Yeaaaa!" Another second, and four hundred women erupted in applause and cheers.

I was speechless.

I noticed one woman in particular. She was beaming with anticipation, much as a child on Christmas morning. The thought of her man's demise seemed to please her, and that scared the hell out of me.

I made a point of saying hello to her after the speech. She was a slender, stylish woman of thirty-five, dressed for success, with an energetic smile and a confident air. She thanked me warmly for my thoughts, saying she found them both provocative and helpful. As we talked, I found that everything about this woman seemed gentle and kind. Yet deep within her, in some mental recess, she harbored a paradoxical death fantasy ("paradoxical" because she did, indeed, love her husband, yet harbored a fantasy about his death). More sobering than this was the realization that she was not alone.

All across America I'd found a similar reaction. When I'd mention the title of my most recent book, *What to Do When He Won't Change*, women of every size and description had reacted with bitterness or cynicism. "I know what to do, kick him out!" "That's easy, divorce the bum!" One woman's bloodletting reaction had caught me off guard: "Eliminate him, and I don't mean leave."

The women in my office were no different. One woman struggled with a husband who refused to discuss their marital troubles. She admitted that she secretly wished her husband's plane would crash during one of his business trips. And there was another woman, who when I noted that her workaholic husband might be heading for a heart attack, simply smiled.

Why are otherwise considerate, loving women engulfed in such bitterness? Depression was my first thought. But these women don't sit around, letting their home, children, and careers deteriorate, I reasoned. If anything, they are take-charge problem-solvers, who bubble with excitement and are quick to help others in distress. After further research, I discovered that, though these women's death fantasies were the most shocking, they certainly were not the most important symptom of their fundamental problem—loneliness; more specifically, they suffered from "Living Together Loneliness," LTL.

Dr. Sigmund Freud spoke of death fantasies as being the product of a person's unconscious death instinct. After listening to the bitterness that loneliness can cause, I can see why the LTL woman wishes, in Dr.

Freud words, "to reduce [her man] to an inorganic state."

Dr. Benjamin Wolman, a well-respected research psychologist, refined Dr. Freud's works by saying that the death wish is not so much an expression of an unconscious death instinct as it is a struggle for survival. I prefer this interpretation when considering the LTL death fantasy.

The LTL woman's death fantasy develops slowly over the course of time. Younger or newly married women don't experience it nearly as often as do older women. The fantasy is most likely to occur in women over thirty-five who've been married at least ten years. Predicting exactly when the fantasy might occur in your life (if it hasn't already) is impossible.

However, if you're an LTL woman between the ages of thirty-five and forty-three, and if you're becoming increasingly bitter about your situation, the death fantasy is just around the corner. Why? Maybe it's because you've been married long enough to know that things aren't going to change unless something drastic happens; maybe it's because you hurt as you watch your children struggle with their own loneliness; or maybe it's because you're at, or near, forty and, as Pippin (from the Broadway musical of the same name) pined, you want your life to be "something more than long."

Most death fantasies are passive in nature; that is, the woman has a split-second thought about some force of nature causing an accident that results in her partner's death. In particularly frustrating situations, or in cases of abuse, the fantasy may be active; that is, the woman sees herself as the instrument of her man's demise.

The death fantasy is childlike. It's rather like the time

in our childhood when we were convinced that our problems would disappear if only our parents would suddenly drop dead. We didn't wish any real harm with our magical thinking; we were just expressing our frustration and helplessness.

The LTL woman is not a homicidal maniac; nor does she really wish harm to anyone (not usually, that is). She's caught in an emotional quagmire and finds momentary solace in a fantasy of retaliation. In reality, she's saying, "Help me, I'm trapped."

Her trap is only one of the several paradoxes she faces. Having a relationship and a secure lifestyle supposedly is *the* answer to loneliness, yet she feels terribly alone. Being successful as a wife, a mother, and a worker is supposed to increase her self-esteem, yet she feels intensely inadequate. Blaming him for his insensitivity supposedly explains away her emotional pain, but it, in fact, makes it worse.

A woman who lives with a man yet feels lonely often blames herself as well as him. She has a home, a family, enough money, and plenty of friends. Why does she feel so alone, desolate, barren? Something must be wrong with her. "I'm an ungrateful bitch" is an often-used internal message of self-recrimination. As her frustration intensifies, it's logical that her helplessness might lead to the fantasy of escape through death.

Though the object of the death-fantasy is her man, I believe that the LTL woman's fantasy is often a projection of feelings she has about herself. That is, many an LTL women will fantasize about *his* demise as a way of coping with the fact that her self-blame has reached a critical point. She wishes for relief for herself more than she wishes for harm for another.

SPIRITUAL BEHAVIORISM

How can this painful process of decreasing self-esteem be reversed? What elements are missing or lost that in turn allow this bitter and chronic loneliness to take hold in a person's life? As I counseled these women it became apparent that the answer to these questions was spiritual as well as clinical.

When I refer to the spiritual nature of loneliness, I'll be following the lead of other experts by defining "spiritual" as that subjective realm in which each person assigns a meaning to his or her life that goes beyond material reality. One aim of this book is to show how developing a practical, inner faith as a basis for living drastically lessens or even eliminates LTL.

Spiritual Behaviorism is a philosophy of psychological treatment that blends the excellence of science with the power of faith. As a counseling method, it gives people the best information that behavioral science has to offer, and then encourages them to use their inner faith to shape that information in a way that fits with their moral values and their unique way of living.

Spiritual Behaviorism requires people to make a leap from external comparisons to internal meaning, from the material to the spiritual world. Lonely people must leap over a gap filled with the fear of failure, role conflicts, bad habits, stifled creativity, and uncertainty. It seems a tall order but the power to make the leap is a part of our human heritage. The behaviorist side of me calls this power the "X factor," because it's unknown to the objective observer. The spiritual side of me calls it the soul.

While much has been written recently about the

mind/body connection, and about how these two separate functions often operate as one, Spiritual Behaviorism emphasizes the *brain/soul* connection. There's a strong interdependence between these two human factors. The brain generates information which the soul uses in arriving at truth. This truth, in turn, then informs the brain and provides guidelines for problem-solving operations.

But when, out of fear, the mind manipulates or avoids this truth, denial sets in that can blind people to the truth that their gut instincts know. It is vital to examine your truth as closely as you can and keep an open mind in order to let the program in this book work for you.

In helping you to heal your loneliness, I'll give considerable information—explanations, instructions, and behavioral guidelines. They will lead you to the very edge of longlasting change. But you'll have to use your soul to leap across your fears and anxieties, making my instructions come alive for you.

This leap requires an act of faith. This faith compels you to believe that you have special powers inside of you. This faith says that *only you* can truly heal your loneliness. Your soul is the ultimate source of guidance and truth.

This leap of faith also depends upon the use of what I'll refer to as mantras. A mantra, a word or phrase repeated silently or aloud, is a self-instructional exercise that uses a behavior to increase spiritual strength. Like any good exercise, a mantra must be designed to meet a person's unique personality. The mantra, "I have the power to change my life," is indeed, an important one. However, you may have to change it slightly—"I have control over my destiny"—in order to make it work for you. When I recommend a mantra, remember to juggle the words, if necessary, to make it suit your needs.

Spiritual Principles

There are three principles that will guide your journey into Spiritual Behaviorism. They are: *Truth, Hope, and Love*.

Truth. All the answers to all your problems lie within you. Your task is to seek the information that will unlock these answers. Another person can only give you knowledge; you must find your own Truth.

Hope. Every human response to any given set of circumstances is initially a healing one. The healing response is always present, though it is sometimes misdirected.

Love. The only reliable path to meaning in life is the construction and maintenance of intimacy between people.

Truth, Hope, and Love are the principles behind Spiritual Behaviorism, and they will sustain you as you study the information in this book. When you take the steps toward designing your own personal solution to loneliness, you will see they are the building blocks to a life that is no longer lonely. Truth will help you discover yourself and honestly assess your situation. Hope is what will nurture you along as you see the exercises working, as self-love and love of others is what will ultimately heal LTL.

Think about these principles later today as you chop the carrots, fill the car with gas, or dictate a memo.

Truth, Hope, and Love. Just because I believe in these principles, doesn't mean that I can tell you that they are *the* absolute, everlasting truth—that would violate the Truth principle. I can only ask you to consider them and remind you that many women have used these principles in healing themselves of their hidden loneliness.

I believe that Spiritual Behaviorism offers each person the opportunity to find peace of mind without falling into the trap of the mumbo-jumbo quick-fix, an unfortunate by-product of our high-tech, low-touch world. It requires you to do some work, but it's not harder than what you're already doing. You simply have to redirect your energy, away from maintaining the same old lonely lifestyle, and toward the establishment of Love and Hope based on *your* inner Truth.

Spiritual Behaviorism is nonsectarian and nontheistic. You don't even have to believe in God to practice this philosophy. It's not Christian, Jewish, Buddhist, Muslim, or Hindi. In fact, it has nothing to do with organized religion, although it is compatible with all religions.

When I left the Catholic seminary after three years, I unfortunately threw the baby of spirituality out with the bath water of organized religion. Happily, I've discovered that I can enjoy the fruits of unbridled spirituality without pledging allegiance to any organization. I ask you to make the same discovery.

In order to profit from Spiritual Behaviorism, all you need is to be a human being who seeks a more peaceful life, free from loneliness. If you are dedicated to a religious sect, all the better. Spiritual Behaviorism will only add to your faith.

THE TREATMENT PROGRAM

Because a lonely feeling is such a subjective experience, and almost never replicates itself, it's impossible to measure loneliness objectively. Consequently, the treatment program must involve some degree of spirituality; that is, asking a person to search for greater meaning in his or her life.

As said above, the treatment prescribed for LTL is built on the theory of *Spiritual Behaviorism*, and its three principles—Truth, Hope, and Love.

Because loneliness causes people to become too reliant upon others, the treatment process for LTL is called the "self-reliance program." Here is a summary of the program's five steps.

Step One: Surrender

- Surrender is a behavioral act in which a person recognizes the temporary superiority of a situation.

- In *all* surrenders, kinesthetics take precedence over verbalizations. In other words, moving your body is more important than moving your mouth.

- Surrender is only the first of five steps. Get acquainted with the other four steps before initiating your surrender.

Step Two: Withdrawal

- Contrary to the word's implicit inference, *withdrawal* is a positive step. It's a spiritual act, encompassing meditation on the three principles of Spiritual Behaviorism.

- During withdrawal, a person embraces her solitude and learns to identify the brain/soul connection.

Step Three: Reevaluation
- Reevaluation is an ongoing process whose goal is to examine one's own expectations and beliefs, and to improve one's general personality traits.

- Increasing self-esteem is the most important of all reevaluation tasks.

Step Four: Reemergence
- During reemergence, trial-and-error learning is used to establish new rules that take the place of the old ones.

- Seven new rules that grow out of the new expectations are proposed (see chapter 9).

Step Five: Discovery
- Through the never-ending discovery process, one gradually comes to understand one's inner Truth.

- The challenge in finding Truth is to ask oneself the right questions and trust one's soul to find the right answers.

UNRESOLVED STRESS

Though to the casual observer, and often to herself, she's a picture of efficiency and positive disposition, the LTL woman is under constant stress. While the research doesn't establish a cause-and-effect relationship,

I believe that many women diagnosed as having eating disorders, phobias, and depression are actually suffering from LTL. They often enter therapy to get help for their psychological distress but, in many cases, they end up working on the wrong problem. If left unattended, their loneliness will eventually take a toll on their physical health.

James Lynch, in his sobering book *The Broken Heart: The Medical Consequences of Loneliness*, concludes that lonely people are unusually susceptible to serious illnesses and premature death. Though he was referring to people with uncoupled loneliness, I believe that his conclusion has even *more* relevance to those who are *Living Together, Feeling Alone*. As I pointed out above, the LTL woman's stress is, in some ways, greater than that of a woman who's simply living alone.

Current medical science supports this contention by recognizing that unresolved stress suppresses the body's immune system. Chronic stress lowers the number of "helper" T cells, one of the body's primary defense systems. With a weakened defense, the body is less able to fight off invading diseases.

If a woman is unable to resolve her loneliness, her frustrations can lead to serious problems. A case in point is the reported rise in the incidence of breast and ovarian cancer. Is this simply a result of better diagnosis? I think not. Rather, I believe that the woman whose love is leading to loneliness must come to grips with a frightening reality: *Her loneliness can kill.*

The five steps just outlined will help you gain insight into *your* unique LTL condition, learn why and how it traps you, and what you can do to cope with it. You will not, however, learn to get rid of *all* loneliness; just the part that immobilizes you. As is the case with anxiety and depression, occasional periods of feeling lonesome are a part of life.

Though I'm speaking to women, I recognize that there are situations where the roles are reversed and men (or both partners) are *Living Together, Feeling Alone*. If you're a man, most of my insights apply to you as well. According to research, it's more difficult for men to admit loneliness, so you may have to study a bit longer to achieve the same results as your female counterpart.

This book is about women who are lonely. Though I'll make reference to "his" behavior, I encourage you *not* to blame him for your loneliness—it'll only make matters worse. Your troubled relationship is a *symptom* of an underlying problem.

As you begin to study your loneliness, don't be surprised if opening the door to your inner thoughts and feelings stimulates anxiety. If you need support, think of me holding out my hand to you, offering a gentle touch. Take it, if you wish. Or wait, if you want; it'll still be there. The image of my hand extended in support is my way of saying, "Everything is going to be okay." And it will be.

1

Living Together Loneliness

JILL was dying inside and didn't know what to do about it. The memories of her last birthday—her thirty-ninth—spent waiting for her husband to get home from working late had already melded with the same memories of previous years. Jill's mental anguish had reached the point where her next birthday—the promising milestone of life-begins-at-forty—felt more like a millstone crushing her spirit.

Her gynecologist had noted that she was a "nervous wreck" and gave her pills for her anxiety. Finding no relief, Jill consulted a psychiatrist, who diagnosed her as depressed and hospitalized her. After being numbed by anti-depressive medications and then forced to examine her bland indifference toward life, Jill left the hospital. She wanted answers, not drugs.

Jill was anxious, but she didn't suffer from anxiety neurosis; she was depressed but depression wasn't her biggest problem. Her central problem was loneliness. But, it wasn't the kind of loneliness we all experience when we miss our friends who've moved away or relatives who have died. It was LTL, and in her case, quite severe.

It's only been within the last ten to fifteen years that loneliness has been studied scientifically. In my opinion, Dr. Letitia Anne Peplau and Dr. Daniel Perlman, researchers at the University of California in Los Angeles, have given the best definition of loneliness, one that I'll use in helping you to understand and cope with LTL. They say that loneliness is *"the emotional response a person has to a perceived discrepancy between expected and achieved levels of social contact."*

In other words, clinical loneliness begins when what you get from other people doesn't satisfy what you expect. This definition permits the professional to identify loneliness as a separate and distinct psychological problem—hence, the notion of *clinical* loneliness.

BEYOND LONESOMENESS

In 1938, Dr. Gregory Zilboorg, a psychoanalyst, noted that missing a friend or someone we love—which he called lonesomeness—was not a chronic state. He said that lonesomeness does not require treatment because the cure is part of the cause. "Life itself, toward which the man who happens to be lonesome always turns, cures him sooner or later by what it has to offer."

Dr. Zilboorg went on to say that loneliness is quite different from lonesomeness. Life does not bring relief to the person with clinical loneliness. The lonely "become low-spirited, somewhat irritable, and feel perhaps ill-treated by fate." He noted that diversions don't satisfy their inner needs. "A feeling of emptiness would pervade and they [lonely persons] would appear to cower and succumb under the burden which is loneliness."

Jill's problem was beyond lonesomeness. She was suffering from clinical loneliness; that is, she perceived a discrepancy between her expected and achieved levels of social contact. More specifically, she *expected* her marriage to give her warmth, belonging, and intimacy; it *achieved* none of these.

Jill's husband, Paul, was a vice-president of sales, making more than $200,000 a year. They had two teenagers and lived in an affluent and prestigious suburb. Jill had an inner feeling of emptiness that money and social diversions could not relieve. Even when Paul spent time at home, he wasn't really with her.

Jill felt that Paul was indifferent to her and their children, that he expected too much of her, and that they didn't talk often enough. Their love-making had been replaced by cold, methodical moments of having sex. The closest they ever came to intimacy was when Jill would scream for attention. Those times, Paul confessed to not knowing why she wasn't satisfied with her lot in life.

When Jill turned to her mother for support (which she eventually learned was a mistake), she was only subjected to rejection. "Don't screw up your marriage like you have everything else" her mother had said. When she protested, her mother was quick to remind her how her lack of child-rearing skills had resulted in two disrespectful children.

Life, itself, didn't cure Jill's loneliness. Her feelings of isolation and emptiness deepened and intensified. She identified with Dr. Zilboorg's analogy by saying that she felt as if an "inner worm" were gnawing at her heart.

A DIAGNOSTIC OVERSIGHT

Why had two physicians incorrectly diagnosed Jill's condition? First of all, LTL does not reach out and grab the objective observer and say, "This person is lonely." While I believe that loneliness is a legitimate psychological problem, it's also a disturbance of one's spiritual life. The unique combination of brain and soul results in a pattern of symptoms that is not only unique to the individual but also takes the form of other, more easily identifiable, problems.

To the professionals who evaluated her, Jill's outward symptoms *appeared* to put her in either the anxiety or depression category. She was nervous and irritable. She complained of feeling empty inside and admitted to questioning why she was alive. These feelings are consistent with anxiety and depression. However, they're also part of clinical loneliness.

Studies have concluded that while loneliness and depression share some common symptoms, there's a fundamental difference between the two. This difference is founded on the fact that loneliness is tied to one's social life, while depression is primarily tied to non-social events. That is, a depressed person will be dissatisfied with many aspects of her life—financial, career, education—while a lonely person will be dissatisfied primarily with the social aspect of her life.

A second reason that Jill was misdiagnosed is that most doctors and therapists are not trained to recognize loneliness as a legitimate psychological diagnosis. Traditionally, loneliness has been seen as a sociological problem, with relief coming from social, not psychological, changes. Conclusive evidence of why this is so can be found in an oversight in the mental health practitioner's bible, the *Diagnostic and Statistical Manual*. Though there are hundreds of possible diagnoses, *there is none for loneliness*.

Third, and most important to my concern here, *Jill did not fit the social profile of a lonely person*. According to a wide range of studies, lonely people tend to be: from lower socio-economic levels, less educated, poor risk-takers, shy and introverted. They are without a special partner in life and blame themselves for this condition. This certainly wasn't Jill.

Jill was married, had a college education, was a successful wife, mother, and worker (legal assistant), maintained a wide-ranging and effective social network, had good self-assertion skills, and carried on a vigorous daily schedule. Hers was almost the opposite of the lonely person's social profile.

The source of these oversights is a singular false assumption that runs throughout the scholarly studies; that is, researchers assume that lonely people are without a special partner, or as one expert put it, are "uncoupled." Recently, a team of Dutch psychologists published a paper in which "missing a partner" was a prerequisite for being lonely, while "with partner" was assumed to be synonymous with the absence of loneliness.

Rubinstein and Shaver, in another paper, "The Experience of Loneliness," report that lonely people have three major complaints: they are alone too much, have no partner, and have to come home to an empty house. There is no mention of the possibility that a person could suffer from clinical loneliness *and* be "attached."

The closest anyone came to mentioning LTL was Dr. David Burns in his book, *Intimate Connections*. Summarizing his research on loneliness he said, "One surprising finding from my research is that being married does not in any way protect you from feeling lonely." However, there's no further mention of this finding, nor is it pointed out that *Living Together, Feeling Alone* is a completely different problem from living alone, feeling alone.

BEING "ATTACHED," BUT LONELY

Jill had complained about being lonely to both doctors. But each had dismissed her symptoms as being the result, not the cause, of her anxiety and depression. I believe that they were wrong.

Jill's social profile didn't support the fact that she was suffering from clinical loneliness. Even if her psychiatrist had been familiar with the latest loneliness research, and even if there was a diagnostic category for loneliness, he still wouldn't have seen her as lonely. After all, he might say, she's "coupled" and therefore, by definition, not lonely.

It's understandable that Jill took the prescribed tranquilizers and then submitted to hospitalization. It's also no surprise that she considered attending an eating disorder clinic (she often missed meals and then binged on sweets) and attending meetings of Alcoholics Anonymous (she drank several glasses of wine almost every evening). While both of these latter resource groups could have helped her, neither struck at the heart of her problem.

Jill was desperate for an answer to the question, "What's wrong with me?"

When I asked Jill if she was lonely, she reacted as if she'd stuck her finger in a light socket. "Oh, God, am I!" She sighed deeply, and immediately began to cry.

After I explained how LTL masquerades as other problems and how difficult it is for a person to admit it, Jill was relieved. She felt validated, happy to know that what she thought was bothering her was indeed, a real problem.

Jill and others like her, along with the professionals who try to help them, need to recognize *three* types of lonely feelings: lonesomeness and the *two* types of clinical loneliness.

Lonesomeness happens to all of us sooner or later, and life eventually cures it. However, clinical loneliness encompasses feelings of isolation and abandonment, anxiety and depression that prove resistant to the potions that life has to offer. In both forms of clinical loneliness, the victim perceives a discrepancy between expected and achieved social contact and suffers from low self-esteem. For the most part, the similarity ends there.

Women with uncoupled loneliness are often shy and introverted; LTL women tend to have good social skills and many friends. The former blame themselves for being lonely; the latter blame their man. Unlike uncoupled women, LTL women have a special confidant. Uncoupled women's bitterness is directed toward life; an LTL woman's bitterness is directed at her man (or men in general) and can reach the point where she entertains a death fantasy. Most apparent, LTL women are "attached" but lonely, a condition that until now has not been studied.

WHY LTL NOW?

In my viewpoint, LTL loneliness has emerged as a problem only within the past twenty years. To understand my sense of psychological history, you must recall the definition of clinical loneliness as: *a person's emotional response to a perceived discrepancy between expected and achieved social contact*.

The key word in this definition is "expected." Fifty years ago, most of our grandmas didn't expect their men to give them intimacy, sharing, and emotional belonging. This doesn't mean that they didn't want it or need it; they simply didn't *expect* it. They may have been disappointed or sad, but without the expectation for closeness, *they didn't experience the very private emotion of loneliness*.

LOSING TOUCH WITH YOUR POWER CENTER

Your brain's power center is the core of your responsibility and self-control. It enables you to take action, to weigh the outcome of those actions, to create new alternatives, doing things you've never done before, and to engage in trial-and-error learning. Then, in concert with your soul, it becomes the wellspring of courage, of hope, of self-confidence, and of risktaking. Your power center is the healthy common-sense part of yourself that this book will lead you back to. It's still in you.

Since I'll be referring to your power center throughout this book, I wish that I could give you a simple and direct exercise that would help you find and activate it. But using your power center to overcome loneliness is not like using it to find a better job. The spiritual component of loneliness requires that you dig inside yourself and design your own solution to loneliness.

I can, however, lend insight to the question, How do I recognize my brain's power center when it's operating? Here are some of the signs:

- You create a new solution to an old problem and you feel a tingle or a surge of excitement that signals a sudden awareness of wellness.

- You catch yourself in the act of arguing or apologizing unnecessarily, and you stop your behavior. Your power center is responsible for this underrated, but very crucial act.

- You see a loved one "dumping" on you, or "pushing your anxiety buttons," and you don't react in your old way. Your power center allows you to take a step back from a situation and watch the *process* of the problem as it unfolds, rather than being swamped by the *content*.

- You're sitting in silence and you have an "ah ha!" experience, gaining insight into a problem. It's like rounding the bend and suddenly seeing the "big picture." You finally stand back, look beyond the trees, and see the forest.

Your power center is strengthened when you make a thoughtful choice, weakened when you blindly follow another's directives or let chance rule your life. It embraces wants and needs, while it challenges have to's and musts. It will support moral directives but only when they're rational. When you lose touch with your power center it rusts. Life is difficult, even painful, because you feel that loss. It's hard to know the Truth, feel Love, and have Hope. The way back to a bright, shiny power center is through your own spiritual connection with yourself, with life, and with other people by way of the five steps.

THE FADING SPIRITUAL COMPONENT
IN OUR LIVES

Several authorities on loneliness refer to a spiritual component that tends to dominate loneliness. Although they all were referring to uncoupled loneliness, their comments apply to LTL.

Jill has what Robert Weiss in his 1973 classic book on loneliness calls an "eerie affliction of [her] spirit." Joseph Hartog and his associates conclude that loneliness is a message from our inner psyche, telling us that we need greater spirituality in our lives. Researchers Raymond Paloutzian and Craig Ellison found that the greater the spiritual well-being of a person, the lower the loneliness.

2

Are You Lonely?/The Stages of LTL

This is the first question loneliness researchers ask. The question is obviously important, but a Yes answer doesn't mean much. Is the person going through a normal period of lonesomeness? Is she shy and introverted, lacking an effective social network of friends? Or, is this person victimized by *Living Together, Feeling Alone*?

The subjectiveness of the loneliness experience makes it practically impossible to measure. If you see someone sitting alone in a movie theater crying, is that person lonely? Maybe, maybe not. If that same person sits on a park bench by herself during a moonlit, romantic evening, is she lonely? You can't tell.

One researcher said that he tried to measure the reactions created by loneliness and he stopped after identifying 184. He didn't even try to determine the infinite number of possible combinations of reactions.

Since emotionally charged persons experience several feelings at once, it's possible that your loneliness is so unique that it's never felt the same way twice, *not even by you*. You can see that measuring it is difficult.

However, in order to give you an overview of the inner experience of loneliness, I've selected the best possible method of helping you answer the question, "Are you lonely?"

MEASURING YOUR LONELINESS

You've probably already made a subjective judgment about whether or not you're a victim of LTL. I wish I could give you a foolproof quiz to help you confirm your first impression. But since I'm exploring uncharted territory, the best I can do is to briefly review how uncoupled loneliness is measured and then introduce you to the survey I use in helping LTL victims evaluate their feelings.

Much of the current information available concerning loneliness comes from the use of a loneliness scale developed and refined by researchers at the University of California at Los Angeles. The UCLA Loneliness Scale has proved itself to be a fairly reliable and valid measure of uncoupled loneliness.

Here are five statements from the UCLA Loneliness scale:

There is no one I can turn to.

I feel left out.

I feel isolated from others.

I am unhappy being so withdrawn.

No one really knows me well.

Women who report that they feel this way often are judged to be lonely. However, because she has good friends and a special confidant, the LTL woman typically answers No to most of these statements. But she's still lonely. The trouble with the UCLA scale is that it's built upon the assumption that "attached" women aren't lonely. As you know, this is not true.

If the LTL woman were to answer these statements *in reference* to her partner, the results would be different. For example, consider these modifications of the items from above:

I can't turn to him when I feel bad.

I feel left out of his life.

I feel isolated from him, even when he's in the same room.

I'm unhappy being shut off from him.

He doesn't really know me well.

If you're an LTL woman, I expect that you would agree with most of these statements. Even so, the measurement of your loneliness is *still* not complete. Though it's certainly a major factor, a failing love life is *not* the cause of your loneliness. Any measurement that points a finger of blame will mislead you and make treatment of your condition only marginally successful. The root of your loneliness is in you, not him.

Survey of Feelings

Three researchers in personality assessment, Joseph Scalise, Earl Ginter, and Lawrence Gerstein, proposed a generic measurement of loneliness. It lists fifty of the most frequent emotions lonely people experience. Since it makes no assumptions about the cause of loneliness, I adapted it to my work with LTL women.

You can use this survey to evaluate your lonely feelings from several perspectives: your life within your relationship, your family, your workplace, your community, or your entire world. For our purposes here, evaluate your feelings *within your relationship*. It may take a few extra moments to give a number to each emotion, so take your time. Your score should reflect how you feel now.

Each adjective describes a feeling. Assign a number between 1 and 10 to each adjective by asking yourself how often and how intensely you feel each of the emotions. A score of 10 means that you feel the emotion regularly and intensely. As your score moves downward, the feeling is less frequent and less intense.

Confused

Withdrawn

Hurt

Abandoned

Angry

Discouraged

Empty

Hollow

Scared

Miserable

Uncertain

Useless

Humiliated

Erratic

Numb

Unloved

Nervous

Sad

Worthless

Broken

Because of the experimental nature of this survey, I can only give you a broad interpretation of your total score. A score of 75 seems to be a starting point. Women with scores from 75 to 100 report being lonely, while those with scores from 100 to 125 say that their loneliness is severe. If your score is over 125, your loneliness interferes with your daily functioning, and treatment should be a top priority.

THE STAGES OF LTL

I've observed five stages of *Living Together, Feeling Alone*. Each corresponds with the feeling that dominates one's emotions during that stage. The five are: Bewilderment, Isolation, Agitation, Depression, and Exhaustion. These stages *tend* to be progressive with age, although many women experience them in a sequence unique to their particular circumstances. You may be bewildered at the same situation that angers your best friend, while she feels isolated under conditions that depress you.

The stages can be considered sequential in that the longer a woman lives with LTL, the greater the likelihood that she'll move through the stages in the order outlined below. Though not exclusive and certainly not representative of all women, the age progression of the loneliness stages are:

Bewilderment	Under 28
Isolation	Ages 28 to 34
Agitation	Ages 35 to 42
Depression	Ages 43 to 50
Exhaustion	Over 50

This age progression depends upon a woman getting married at the average age of twenty-two and staying in that marriage. Many things can alter this scheme—divorce, intensity of self-blame, premarital experience, and history of denial, to name a few. The most consistent stage in the age progression is agitation, with onset occurring during the mid- to late-thirties in women who've been married twelve to fifteen years.

A review of each stage will make your self-study more successful.

Bewilderment

LTL usually begins with a sense of bewilderment. "What's going on here?" and "This can't be happening to me" are common thoughts. Abby, a twenty-four-year-old counselor-in-training, had been married to twenty-six-year-old Justin for two years. Her bewilderment depended upon the time of day.

Abby would awaken with a sense of renewed hope, believing that last night's despondency was only the nagging noise of physical exhaustion. She'd remember how nasty Justin was in criticizing her manner of speech, but explain it away by saying that he'd eventually grow up. She would smile as she fixed her hair, validating all the people who ever told her that being married was tough. She'd dismiss her concerns by blaming herself for getting mad at him, and by vowing to do a better job of pleasing him. She'd begin her daily routine convinced that today would be different.

By midday, a familiar sense of uneasiness had crept back into Abby's otherwise sunny disposition, gnawing at her like a nasal tickle preceding a sneeze. She'd realize that today's apprehension about her marriage was no different from yesterday's, or the day before that. A friend might stop by her table for a lunchtime chat, but Abby would be curt and discourteous. The friend would think that Abby was worried about work or school. In truth, she was beginning to experience *alienation*; that is, a feeling of being cut off from the warmth of honest human contact.

Dinnertime was often the worst. Abby would reach out to Justin for some type of emotional embrace, but he would tune her out in favor of the television. She'd try to express her confusion, but it came out as bitterness and would result in a horrendous argument. She'd retreat to her bedroom and try to blame him, but that didn't work either. She was feeling the first hint of what would eventually become the most painful stage of LTL—agitation.

By the time she crawled into bed, Abby was once again exhausted, emotionally more than physically. Her loneliness had begun to depress her. Sadly, the cycle would begin again tomorrow morning.

Isolation

Feelings of isolation, and the resultant alienation, dominate the second stage of LTL. The isolated woman becomes increasingly aware of some type of invisible wall between her and her man. "Sometimes, I see him as a stranger" and "I feel out of tune with him" are common complaints of the isolated woman.

Since her wedding day, isolation had slowly crept into Laura's life. A vivacious and outgoing thirty-seven-year-old woman, Laura had been married to forty-year-old Kevin for three years. It was her first marriage, Kevin's second. They had no children.

Laura was only vaguely aware of the damage that isolation was doing to her personality. Her smile was forced, her laughter scripted, and her Thank You's said with a plastic intimacy. She had a feeling of social estrangement, even with her best friend. She was experiencing the psychological distance that's part of the isolation stage of LTL. It wasn't until she started suffering headaches that her denial started to crumble.

Laura's alienation was a harrowing experience. It robbed her of her sense of self and, in light of Kevin's unwarranted criticisms, convinced her that *she* was failing as a marital partner.

Alienation is often considered an indication of mental illness, an assumption that's not necessarily true. When "normal" people become alienated, they use *technical* rather than *personal* communication.

When Laura went to the butcher, she'd say, "The beef you gave me last week was good." This is a technical communication. An example of a personal communication would be, "I enjoyed the beef you gave me last week." "The dinner was good and the music enjoyable" is technical; "I loved the food and music last evening" is personal. The fundamental difference between the two forms of communication is that technical communication doesn't have a sense of self. This is the hallmark of alienation.

"When Kevin talks to me," Laura said, "I get the feeling that he looks right through me. Sure, we discuss something, but it's so mechanical, so logical."

"What do you do?" I asked.

"We talk for a few minutes. I try to give him my opinion but he always seems to make the final decision. Then, we go on with our lives."

"Don't you voice your feelings?"

"I used to, but we'd just argue. And, as you already know, I can't stand arguing. He'd just say that I was getting emotional. So, I quit it."

Laura's desire to please Kevin became self-defeating. She gave up her friends because *he* didn't like them, and suspended her favorite pastimes because he was jealous of her absence. When she was with Kevin, Laura backed away from her feelings. She had systemically taught herself not to let her personal reactions enter into a conversation with her man. In essence, she had crushed her own spirit.

Laura traced her isolated feelings to Kevin's insensitivity, and believed that her loneliness was caused by her frustrated love life. She didn't look beyond her relationship in seeking an answer to LTL. This was a mistake.

Agitation

Clark Moustakes, in his book *Loneliness*, says that "Aggressiveness often is a disguise of loneliness and may be expressed as cynicism or contempt for men." Later, he reasons that the lonely individual "reveals an excessive and repressed sentimentality and experiences immense anxiety that his [her] weakness will be exposed."

This was said of uncoupled loneliness. I've discovered that cynicism and contempt dramatically increase when a woman lives with a man in what's supposed to be a loving relationship, but, in fact, is characterized by ostracism and isolation.

"I've become a bitch," JoAnn said, taking time out from complaining about her husband to give herself this burning self-indictment. JoAnn, thirty-five, had been married to forty-year-old Spencer for thirteen years, and was gradually becoming aware of the intensity of her loneliness.

When asked why she considered herself a bitch, JoAnn gave an example.

"The other day," she said, "I asked Spence why he had such a long face and he said that he was depressed. I really let him have it. He asked me, 'Why don't people like me?' I said, 'People don't like you because you're an asshole!' And that wasn't enough. Then, I told him that he acted like an asshole because his mom and dad were lousy parents. Then, I told him that he treated me like an asshole and that's the reason I'm so nervous.

"I have a side of me that's a mean, nasty little girl, and I don't like myself when she comes out. She can be so cruel, it's like a dark side of me takes over. I know how much his parents mean to him, and I knew exactly how to hurt him. But I was just fighting back. He takes delight in making me feel bad, so I just had to say it."

After thirteen years of declining intimacy, and increased distance from her own power center, it was understandable that JoAnn became revengeful. However, the more she tried to blame Spencer for her anguish, the worse it became. Like so many LTL women at the agitation stage, JoAnn found it difficult to let go of the past and enjoy the moment.

JoAnn could remember many instances in which she had felt slighted by Spencer. There was last Christmas when he spent the entire day watching television and ignored her sister and brother-in-law. There was her tenth high school reunion when he flirted with the "slut," Betty Johnson, JoAnn's old nemesis. Then, there was the embarrassment that she felt during their wedding reception when he tried to get "too friendly" with one of the bridesmaids.

Whenever Spencer showed the slightest insensitivity, JoAnn dug into her memories, pulled out an example of his past sins, and bluntly rubbed his face in it. Spencer became defensive, which only gave JoAnn more opportunity to remind him what an awful person he'd always been. Sadly for JoAnn, these revenge tactics, born of agitation, hurt her more than they did her husband. JoAnn had lost the ability to do those things her power center enabled her to do—take a leap of faith, create positive solutions, break out of old habits.

During this stage, the LTL woman seriously considers divorce. Her agitation, coupled with alienation, may also generate a death fantasy. If and when she becomes aware of the fantasy, she silently condemns herself even further, and starts to believe that she really might be disturbed.

Depression

Faced with continual sadness and disappointment, it's inevitable that some of LTL woman's anger will turn inward and she'll become depressed. Her symptoms may include irritability, poor concentration, an eating or a sleep disturbance, and a feeling that life is not worth the struggle.

Thirty-three-year-old Kris had one "blue day" after another. The attractive, blond housewife was irritable and restless. She still thought that life was worth living; she just wasn't very good at living it. Her major complaint was that she'd mysteriously lost the boundless energy she used to have.

While there was no doubt that Kris was depressed, it wasn't her *primary* problem; loneliness was. Each time I asked her about one of her complaints, the conversation moved back to her lousy marriage. Her depression was limited to the lack of intimacy in her relationship. This placed her in the depression stage of LTL.

As so often happens, Kris' depression was a sign of resignation, of being beaten. Emptiness had become such a constant companion in her life, that she *used* depression to dull her pain.

Exhaustion

If you've had your spirit crushed by confusion and isolation, your warmth destroyed by agitation, and your hopes dashed by depression, you'll eventually become emotionally exhausted. If your anger and depression don't force you to confront your loneliness, it's predictable that you'll end up feeling a loss of vigor, resourcefulness, and effectiveness. You'll feel as if you have no energy. Or, as forty-nine-year-old Helen said, "I feel dead inside."

Helen had grown up in an impoverished home. Being the most self-sufficient of six children, she was ignored most of the time. Without guidance and encouragement, Helen had when she was young developed all the signs of uncoupled loneliness. She was shy and introverted with a low self-esteem; had a poor social network and no special confidant; suffered a chronic state of isolation, with loneliness starkly unchanged day after day; was unwilling to take risks; had constant fantasies about having a special partner; and felt unyielding self-blame for her loneliness.

Helen, who worked as an office manager for a car dealership, had married Bernie four months after she met him in a Bible study class. Bernie had also lacked social skills, but Helen thought he could have been an owner of a Dale Carnegie franchise for all her experience.

Though Bernie was distant and rarely made love to her, Helen believed that, after so many years, her loneliness was finally over. Unbeknownst to her, it was about to enter another phase.

Over the years, Helen both worked and cared for Bernie and their two children. Whenever Helen was tempted to complain about Bernie's demanding, insensitive ways, she blamed herself for being ungrateful.

"If I want to talk to him about something," Helen said, "or ask him a question, I have to walk into the family room, wait until there's a commercial on the television, and then speak. But if he wants something, he yells at me to come to the family room right then. If I hesitate, he screams at me."

I thought Helen might start crying, but she sat and stoically gazed past me to an abstract painting on the wall. Finally, she spoke, apparently after having carefully considered Bernie's demanding behavior. "It seems to me that this is not equal."

Helen's exhaustion caused her to play nursemaid to a man who obviously needed to grow up. Sure, when push came to shove, Helen knew that Bernie's behavior was not only "not equal," but also was way out of line. She was just too tired to do anything about it.

Though exhausted, Helen was not ready to give up.

If she were, she would've cried "uncle" years ago. So, she went on, somewhat blindly, more out of habit than desire. Why did she do it? Because she always had. And, in the final analysis, she ended up right back where she started—bewildered.

The stages of LTL are often modified by the "passages" that women encounter. Child-bearing and the nurturing instinct stimulate an optimism that, when continually frustrated, can turn to bewilderment and agitation. When your children no longer need you, and you turn to your failing relationship for attachment, isolation and depression can result. The normal ebbing of your energy level and slowing of your metabolic system correlates with feelings of exhaustion. Add to these, the stress of disease, social mobility, and the death of loved ones, and you can see how the stages of LTL can quickly overlap and lose the nice-and-neat look I've tried to give them.

SURVEY OF STAGES

Only a few minutes have passed since you surveyed your lonely feelings. However, *they've already changed.* That's the nature of loneliness. One moment's experience is never duplicated. It and the emotions you felt are gone. Now, your loneliness will manifest itself in a slightly different way.

You can demonstrate the ever-changing nature of your lonely feelings by retaking the survey from yet another perspective. I've organized the feelings according to the stages during which they are most likely to hit a peak (all the feelings can appear some or all of the time, and in varying degrees).

Following the same procedure, retake the survey.

Bewildered

    Confused

    Discouraged

    Uncertain

    Erratic

Isolated

    Unloved

    Abandoned

    Useless

    Empty

Agitated

    Angry

    Nervous

    Humiliated

    Scared

Depressed

    Sad

    Worthless

Hurt

Miserable

Exhausted

Withdrawn

Numb

Broken

Hollow

This time, add up your scores by stages, so that you have five different scores, each with a maximum total of 40. Any score over 20 indicates a problem in that category; scores over 30 suggest that the problem is serious.

YOUR LONELINESS PROFILE

I suggest that you keep a diary monitoring your loneliness. In the beginning, survey your feelings once or twice a day. Later on, once or twice a week will be sufficient. Record your findings by stage, and note any major shifts in emotions. Do not sit and ruminate on what you've found. Excessive self-study can be worse than no self-study at all, because it stimulates self-pity, one of the most debilitating of all human conditions.

Carla's Loneliness. Carla was a thirty-four-year-old, auburn-haired flight attendant. Her happy-go-lucky outlook on life was infectious. Recently, however, her mood had turned somber, and her friends and co-workers were worried about her.

Carla had started drinking too much and flirting with members of the cockpit crew, two things that she'd always been critical of in others. She made cynical or outright hostile remarks about Jake, her thirty-eight-year-old husband.

Carla had been twenty when she married the first time, more to get away from home than because she was in love. Her first husband had a long string of girlfriends, and she finally divorced him. She'd been happily single for six years before marrying Jake.

Carla's feeling profile was one of the highest I'd ever recorded:

Bewilderment	36
Isolation	26
Agitation	40
Depression	31
Exhaustion	35

It is quite rare for a woman of Carla's age and experience to have such high scores in each category. One possible explanation for this rarity is that she was in her second marriage. She was bewildered and isolated because a relatively new marriage was failing. She was agitated and depressed because she viewed this failure as an ominous sign that she'd never find love. The two marriages combined with a troubled childhood gave her a sense of premature exhaustion.

If your lonely feelings fluctuate from day to day, try

not to let it frustrate you. Realize that you're strong enough to tolerate this state of flux and remind yourself that, once you get through these next few months using the simple stages outlined in this book, you'll never again be victimized by such crushing loneliness.

If you are a woman who lives with a special partner but feels alone, do yourself a favor and put thoughts of leaving on the back burner. Turn inward and study your loneliness. Lonesomeness can be "cured" from the outside, but loneliness will pursue you until you cure yourself from the inside.

Whatever your age and stage, LTL has probably already eroded your confidence and self-esteem. To recover, you must thoroughly understand your loneliness, why it developed, and how to escape it.

Perhaps you now recognize in yourself a discrepancy between what you expected your life to be and the way it really is. Perhaps you relate to Carla, who felt there was a hole in her heart. You can heal that wound by finding your way back to your power center through Spiritual Behaviorism.

3

External Causes of LTL

THERE are two elements outside of yourself that help trigger the *Living Together, Feeling Alone* experience: the culture in which the loneliness occurs and the isolating behavior of your partner. These elements begin a chain reaction that culminates in the most basic of all lonely feelings—emptiness.

CULTURE AND SOCIETY

As you'll recall, loneliness is the emotional response a person has to a perceived discrepancy between expected and achieved levels of social contact. Some of these expectations are our own private inventions, but many of them come from the world around us. We learn about our roles from parents, relatives, and teachers, but we are also strongly influenced by books, films, and other media. We *expect* our lives to *achieve* whatever we see around us being regarded as "normal." And no one ever discussed whether June Cleaver (Beaver's sit-com Mom) was lonely.

Our culture is the sum total of our mores, beliefs, institutional practices, arts, and all other thoughts and procedures that shape how we live. Several critical issues that concern the problem of LTL are reviewed below. These are not given as excuses to be lonely but, rather, as a framework for understanding your particular loneliness.

Women's Changing Roles

The women's movement has been a major contributor to the change in expectations that women have concerning themselves and their place in society. Feminism broke old taboos, created new possibilities, and thrust many women into a massive role conflict. Women who reached maturity in the late sixties and early seventies were particularly torn. While cultural conditioning pushed them toward the old way—subservience, the new expectations pulled them toward the new way—equal opportunity and respect.

"Femininity" became an anomaly, a hotly contested, everchanging concept. In this time of great transition and few role models, even younger women with adventuresome spirits looked at the confusing expectations for women and asked, "Am I doing this right?"

Expectations about child-rearing began to change as Moms who stayed home became Moms who worked outside the home. Mothers now were being told that they didn't need to spend so much time supervising their offspring at the risk of "smothering" them. The dishwasher, frozen foods, and other high-tech marvels further idled/liberated the American woman.

Mobility

Corporate wives are the new migrant workers. They sweat and toil for their partner's advancement, and then, with little warning, must pull up stakes and move on to a new city. They get so used to sacrificing friends, neighborhood, and a sense of community that they get antsy if they stay in one place longer than two years.

Corporate wives discover that corporations pay little, if any, attention to how mobility affects family members. Women, typically, are expected (by their husbands *and* by themselves) to promote peace and tranquility during the transition, no matter what the price.

They have to find the doctor, the dentist, the best grocery store, the schools, the church, the pharmacy, not to mention having to arrange and to supervise the endless services a household needs during and after a move. But, it's not just the logistical aspects of the move that cause the problem. The real cause of the problem is the socioemotional factors of the move. Not only must she endure the absence of friends, neighbors, and comfortable routines, the woman must also confront a mate's new expectations at work as well.

High-Tech, Low Touch

If Dr. Abraham Maslow's theory of the hierarchy of needs is correct, we are a nation of people who take food, shelter, and safety for granted and now crave belonging. And, if the researchers are correct, concern about belonging stimulates an increase in loneliness. So, as we turn our attention away from the physical and to the psychological, we increase our chances of becoming lonely.

Our high-tech achievements have given most of us a much more comfortable lifestyle. However, there's a severe psychological cost to our achievements. We've forgotten that true belonging is achieved through gentle, unfettered encounters, as we touch each other in love; that it's not manufactured in mass quantity by an instant gratification machine that turns out plastic intimacy.

In gaining power over nature, we've been seduced into a destructive ego trip. We see ourselves as no longer a part of the natural order or subject to the laws of nature. We no longer see that we need touching, both spiritual as well as physical. We begin to think of ourselves as infallible; we become alienated from the truth inside ourselves, and enamored with the material world around us.

Freedom's Trap

Dr. Eric Fromm's book *Escape from Freedom* is a masterpiece. The centerpiece of this work is Dr. Fromm's contention that, under certain conditions, freedom becomes a trap from which a person wishes to escape. This work has never been more relevant than in today's culture, in which freedom is considered a god.

By definition, freedom entails the availability of options for behavior. The greater the number and the scope of the options, the greater the freedom. Freedom becomes a trap at the point when these options become so complicated that the person's choice creates more problems than it solves.

Take divorce, for example. Fifty or sixty years ago, divorce was not a realistic option for many women. Now, because of social recognition, improved financial circumstances, and modified religious viewpoints, divorce is an option that many women are free to choose.

As is always the case, increased freedom brings added responsibility. Getting divorced can lead to budgetary restraints, child-rearing problems, dating nightmares, and sexually transmitted diseases, not to mention the possibility of uncoupled loneliness. It's not, as so many women are learning, the ticket to unencumbered freedom.

Dr. Fromm's assertion has a special application to the issue of LTL. While all women are faced with complicated decisions about marriage, motherhood, and career advancement, LTL women have a special problem. They face the mind-boggling task of discriminating between lonesomeness and loneliness, between constructive criticism and bullying, between empathy and pity, and between times for reflection and times to get on with life.

As they struggle to maintain their inner balance, weighing their needs against their responsibilities, they inevitably ask themselves, "When does my self-love become self-ish?" Without an answer, self-alienation results, quickly followed by loneliness.

If the social theorists are correct, we're still in a time of cultural transition. As we move from the old to the new, we will look for stable feelings of belonging in an unsettling world. For some women, the transition has been easy; many more have found it difficult. The conflict between old roles and new expectations generates a power imbalance; that is, a woman's power to change the quantity of her life—money, access, authority—has outdistanced her power to change the quality of her life—self-esteem, respect, self-confidence. Her social power is far ahead of her psychological power. The major fallout of this discrepancy is a sense of being out of step with others, of being left behind. Loneliness is often the result.

HIS ISOLATING BEHAVIOR

When a partner behaves in an insensitive manner, the LTL woman can easily feel cut off from his love. However, his actual behavior isn't as important as how she *perceives* his actions *at that moment*. (Such isolating behavior, when acted out by other loved ones, such as parents, siblings, or children, plays a secondary role in the LTL experience, as we will see later.)

If you see your partner as isolative, his intentions are not as important as your feelings, at least not at the outset. Even if a thousand psychologists were to agree that you misread your partner's actions, *it would not make any difference*. If you saw him as insensitive, and felt isolated, that's good enough. Your perception is primary.

A person is particularly vulnerable to the isolative behavior of a partner because of the nature of human bonding. When we bond with another person, we let down our guard, and expose our inner selves, including our weaknesses. We consciously go against the natural instinct of self-protection because of the higher good that we can, and need to, achieve—intimacy and belonging.

As you take a look at the isolative behaviors that you may encounter, remember to take responsibility for your own actions and reactions. See what his behavior triggers in *you*, not why *he* acts as he does. If you think, "I'm lonely because of how he acts," then you've lost touch with your power center. If some of these scenarios sound familiar to you, you will be able to build them into your self-reliance program later.

Refusing to Talk

It's very frustrating to sit with your man, try to talk with him, and have him respond as if you're a nuisance.

You reach out to him and he snaps at you. Something's obviously bothering him but he won't tell you. An hour later you overhear him on the phone telling his best friend about a work problem, or you're at a party and his secretary asks you if your husband's father will have to go to the hospital. You didn't even know his father was sick.

One partner refusing to talk to another is a veiled act of hostility. The implicit message is, "I'm mad at you so I'm shutting you out." If the LTL woman is especially sensitive to rejection, she may immediately think, "What did I do wrong?" This self-blame makes it nearly impossible for her to remember that refusing to talk is indicative of *his* problem.

On the other side of the coin, remember that silence between you and your partner can indicate a strong relationship (for example, sitting together in the same room without speaking). You're at peace with each other and though you don't talk, you're still communicating. This is a delicious moment of solitude.

Demanding

You're busy in one part of the house and he yells, demanding that you get him something or come to where he's sitting. The demanding partner who tries to tell you what to do (how to dress, what to cook) subjugates you to his whims.

His friends come over all the time and you're expected to provide snacks. Even his friends become demanding, telling you, "Get me a beer." It might be a little easier to take if your partner showed some appreciation or helped out once in a while.

It's natural to get angry at being treated as a servant. But if you're afraid of your anger, you'll likely shy away from confrontation. This, in turn, will promote depersonalization, characteristic of the early stages of *Living Together, Feeling Alone*. There can be no substitute for being treated with dignity and respect. To mindlessly comply with a demanding partner insures loneliness.

Ostracism of Friends

It's one thing when he expects you to wait on his friends, quite another when he belittles, ignores, or otherwise ostracizes your friends. When he's jealous of the time you spend with others, you're being forced to cut off contact with your social network.

Many LTL women submit to these expectations early on because they think it's a temporary adjustment to the relationship, or because they feel honored that he "wants me to himself." However, more often than not, such submission represents the activation of the old, ineffective rule that tells you to maintain peace at any price.

Constant Criticism

A more active form of ostracism is constant criticism. Dinner's late, his bowling shirt is wrinkled, the towels smell funny, your mother's too nosy, you were mean to his father last weekend, the car's dirty, and the kids are spoiled. His part in these things is never mentioned.

My research says that this hypercriticism began before living together and intensified during the first year of cohabitation. The woman's low self-esteem is the flaw in her that permits this type of emotional abuse to continue. This is complicated by the fact that a woman with a long history of being unduly criticized (going back to her childhood), may not have enough self-esteem to mount an effective confrontation. Outside support is usually called for.

Sexual Abuse

Because gentle touching is the most powerful and immediate antidote for loneliness, you can imagine how isolating it feels when a touch is used in a cold, self-centered, or cruel fashion. To stimulate loneliness, sexual abuse doesn't have to be physical.

Admitting a mistake so that he can get sex, paying no attention to your sexual needs, and belittling you sexually are all abusive acts that can result in loneliness. However, such alienation cannot occur in women who have an active power center and a healthy self-love.

Emotional Vacancy

The isolating man's opinion about feelings is that, "they're more trouble than they're worth." One lonely woman reported that her man had said, "Feelings just get in the way. They don't have any use." He was an emotionally vacant person.

The women I've seen endure this type of isolating behavior have been afraid of rejection. Whether because of immaturity or a troubled childhood, they failed to trust their emotions and relied, instead, upon some vague notion of "how things have always been." Without incorporating a balance of reason and emotion, they're destined to constantly fail, never understanding why.

A relationship devoid of emotional sharing is like a beautiful car with no gas. Sharing feelings is the fuel that keeps a relationship moving, carrying each partner into new interpersonal territory. Emotionally vacant relationships lose their power quickly, and each partner's concern for the other rolls backward downhill.

Blaming Others

If your partner doesn't want to take his share of the responsibility for the relationship, he'll blame you, or someone else, for failures and setbacks. "We wouldn't have to spend one hundred dollars on the television if you'd done something sooner." "You should have let me handle the lawn instead of employing some high school dropout." "Why didn't you tell me that the teacher was flunking our kid, I would've taken care of it?"

Facts are: You mentioned the fuzzy reception on the television months ago; he said he would mow the grass but "never got around to it"; he pays little or no attention to his son's report card and never goes to parent-teacher conferences. But he doesn't remember these facts because he rarely, if ever, listens to you.

The woman whose partner blames her for everything probably thinks he is right. Her tendency toward self-blaming makes her vulnerable to his finger-pointing. This condition can easily trigger any "abandonment complex" a woman might be carrying around inside her unconscious mind.

False Contrition

"I'm sorry that we had a problem" and "I'm sure that I was wrong, I'm human aren't I?" are two of his verbal behaviors that sound positive but can be representative of a false contrition. He sounds as if he wants to come closer to you, but, in fact, you feel lonelier.

If your man appears contrite whenever he wants something from you, he's probably a master of false contrition.

Nurturance Rejected

Since part of belonging is the giving as well as receiving of love, the LTL woman's loneliness can be dramatically increased if her partner rejects her attempts to nurture him. She tries to rub his neck, but he flips her hand away. She offers empathy for his work stress, and he snaps, "Leave me alone."

The isolated LTL woman may overlook the fact that her partner rejects the love she tries to give him. She sees it as just more evidence that she must do a better job of pleasing him. When your man doesn't need you, you can easily conclude that your love is faulty.

THE ISOLATING BEHAVIORS OF OTHER LOVED ONES

While your man is the primary catalyst of your loneliness, I may have inadvertently given you the idea that he's the *only* one who can trigger a feeling of isolation. While the LTL experience requires that you perceive isolation coming from your partner, there are other loved ones who can add to your loneliness. Let's look briefly at three of them.

Your Teenager. A rebellious teenager has an endless variety of ways of telling his parents how useless they've become. This is especially true of pubescent boys toward their mothers. If your self-esteem is already low, or you're struggling with the peace-at-any-price philosophy, the heartless attack of your headstrong teenager can intensify the LTL experience.

Your Sibling. Most brothers and sisters look to each other for a sense of familial support. Even when they don't approve of what a brother does, or how a sister talks, the blood-is-thicker-than-water rule seems to hold true. If and when you turn to one of your siblings for a sense of belonging, and he or she rejects you or unduly criticizes you, your isolation will likely increase.

Your Parents. Nearly all of the women I've worked with have endured some type of rejection from one or both of their parents. Parental rejection cuts with a double edge. The parents who reject you today are often the same ones who originally taught you the ineffective rules that support the LTL experience.

Though they appear to be the most direct causes of LTL, the culture and his isolating behaviors are not as critical as they appear. The internal causes, or the hidden ones, are much more important and deserving of your careful attention.

4

Internal Causes of LTL

Now that you know (although you may not feel connected to your power center yet) that your healing process begins with you (not your mate, your marriage, or your mother-in-law), it's time for some honest self-examination. There are no quizzes and no scores in this section, just examples of women you might relate to. Remember, you must be prepared to find your way back to *your* Truth, even though there might be some difficult passages along the way. Let your power center go back to work for you!

There are two elements *inside* of you that have a direct impact on the LTL experience: your personality shortcomings and the role conflict that develops when old rules clash with new expectations.

PERSONALITY SHORTCOMINGS

A personality shortcoming is a general trait that represents a glitch in your philosophy of life. There are four personality shortcomings that provide the foundation of LTL: *low self-esteem* or "I'm inadequate," *powerlessness* or "I can't do anything about my situation," *narcissism* or "I'm responsible for everyone's problems," and *fear of anger* or "Anger is not permissible."

His isolating behavior, then, acts as a spark to trigger your personality shortcomings. Within seconds after his comment, a variation of the following statement streaks through your mind: "I'm an inadequate person (low self-esteem) because I cause him to treat me this way (narcissism), but I can't do anything about it (powerlessness), including getting angry (fear of anger)." The stronger this belief, the greater the impact his isolating behavior will have upon you.

Low Self-Esteem

Self-esteem is the sum total of the positive and negative things that you say about yourself—that is, your self-referencing. If your self-referencing is decidedly negative, you'll suffer from low self-esteem. While self-esteem is sexless (i.e., both men and women possess it), it manifests itself differently in women than in men. In LTL, low self-esteem is both proactive and reactive: that is, it existed *before* the LTL condition developed, and is worsened by the condition itself.

Many women aren't aware of their low self-esteem. Fran was a case in point.

Fran, a forty-five-year-old, thickset woman, had been married for twenty-one years to forty-seven-year-old Norman. They had two children, ages fourteen and nine. Fran was working as a part-time day care worker and Norman owned a printing business.

Despite her outer gruffness, Fran was a very gentle woman. Her parents had owned a nursery, and she'd spent much of her childhood helping them care for the plants and flowers they raised. She remembers sneaking away during her parents' endless arguments, and sitting in the family's greenhouse, nestled softly in the lush foliage of the broadleaf philodendrons.

Fran portrayed herself as a self-confident woman. However, two pieces of nonverbal data helped me to see through the masquerade. First, she spoke in a cold, mechanical way, obviously trying to detach herself from her real feelings. Second, each time she used a personal pronoun (I, me, my, mine), a slight sneer crossed her lips. "Fran" was obviously a distasteful subject to her. It would take time for her to confront her low self-esteem, so I moved slowly.

Fran didn't develop her low self-esteem by accident. Her mom had been a grim taskmaster and nothing Fran ever did was good enough. "Why can't you do it right the first time?" her mother would say sarcastically. Although she remembers her father as a "sad, but nice man," he was, in fact, an alcoholic who never failed to take advantage of other people, including Fran.

Fran's low self-esteem had damaged her ability to love. From the first moment of their courtship, Fran thought herself unworthy of Norman's affection. As their love bloomed, self-recrimination slowly crept into her daily life. She blamed herself for her children's bad grades, her mother's complaints (though she was a caring daughter), and her inability to protect Norman from his own mother's icy rejection. In some part of her inner consciousness, she even blamed herself for those times when Norman was insensitive. "If I loved him correctly,'' her inner voice would say, ''he wouldn't treat me this way.''

Thinking negative thoughts about yourself can easily lead to social and emotional withdrawal. You push yourself into isolation, not wishing to let other people see the lousy person that you think you are.

''I'm undesirable'' and ''I'm dull and boring'' are two other self-references that the LTL woman uses to define herself. More often than not, she thinks that *he's* thinking these things. If her self-esteem is quite low, it won't make any difference if her partner denies such thoughts. She'll think that he's just trying to protect her feelings.

Fran's low self-esteem caused her to have an exaggerated sense of responsibility; that is, when something went wrong, she rushed to take responsibility for it. She saw herself as such a lousy person that she must have caused the problem. Low self-esteem had become such a way of life that a compliment was viewed as an intrusion, almost an assault, upon her identity.

Self-condemnation further lowers one's self-esteem as it triggers anger. The anger embodies the woman's attempt to take the blame away from herself and place it somewhere else. And, if for no other reason than being a flawed human being, her partner will give her ample opportunity to dump her anger. But, because her anger is caused by low self-esteem, and not his behavior, the dumping never works.

In many cases, the LTL woman's low self-esteem is complicated by a strange irony. That is, her low self-esteem is often confined to how she thinks about herself in relationship to her man. Thirty-eight-year-old Marilyn had that problem.

Marilyn was a rental manager with no children. She was the prototype of social competence. She was vice-chairperson of the League of Women Voters and past-president of the local businesswomen's organization. Her social grace wasn't a masquerade. She was respected by her friends and acquaintances and, usually, by herself.

But take her away from a business setting and put her at home with her husband, Jerry, and she suddenly became a different person. She was a nervous pile of insecurities whose theme seemed to be, "He's okay and I'm a failure!"

The moment she walked through the door of her home, her confidence disappeared in a barrage of negative self-references. The old subservience role reared its head and demanded that she cook, clean, and do her man's bidding. The discrepancy between what she expected and achieved at work and at home is obvious. Wanting to *do* the housework was not Marilyn's problem—feeling insecure about her ability to be good at it was.

Along with a paycheck, the modern woman gains self-esteem from her job. She gets to battle successfully with the corporate "big boys." But if she's not careful, when she walks through the door of her house she'll suddenly be shoved into another world. There, all the old childhood admonitions will come rushing back, now sounding like a legion of ghosts.

Lessons About Low Self-Esteem

- Low self-esteem is the result of deficient learning. You're not bound forever by what happened to you in your childhood. You can overcome it.

- Your low self-esteem originated *before* you began living with a man. Don't blame him for it.

Fear of Anger

Have you ever noticed that men have a difficult time recognizing and coping with their fears? Or that women, on the other hand, have a similar problem with anger? You might say that men are angry about their fears, and that women are afraid of their anger.

Because she has been conditioned not to express her anger, the LTL woman keeps denying it until she gets so angry that she's ready to explode. Vivian's story is a perfect example.

Thirty-six-year-old Vivian couldn't see the forest for the trees. Though bright and socially aware, Vivian was trapped in an abusive relationship. Her father had treated her like a nonperson, and her husband, Jack, picked up where her father had left off.

Jack could have set a record for insensitivity. He counted the money from the reception rather than make love with her on their wedding night. He went bowling the night that their first baby was due. He never held the children or helped care for them. He would pick on her the moment he got home. "Why isn't dinner cooked?" "Why didn't you get the dryer fixed?" "I asked you to get my shoes cleaned." After dinner, he would fall asleep on the couch and demand not to be awakened for any reason. If the kids accidentally woke him up, he would yell at them.

"The one thing that absolutely dumbfounds me," I said inquisitively, "is why you do it. Why do you continue living with a man you describe as clearly abusive, if not mentally disturbed?"

"I sincerely don't know," she said. "Don't think I haven't asked myself that same question over and over again." She had become so distanced from her power center that her own truth was difficult to find.

She thought for a moment, then, with a quizzical tone, continued. "I feel sorry for him and I guess my purpose is to protect myself from his anger."

"You stay with Jack," I said, making more of a question than a statement, "because you're afraid of his anger. What does that mean?"

"If I leave him or kick him out, I'm afraid of what he might say."

"Would he hurt you?"

"No," she said directly. "But he would really get mad."

"What happens when he gets mad?"

"It usually occurs after he's been drinking," she said. "He starts picking on the kids, screaming at me, and complaining about everything. I don't even want to think what he'd do if I signed the divorce papers."

"And, if he 'came off the wall,' so to speak, what *would* you do?"

"I have a very strong feeling," she said, looking at me intensely, "that I wouldn't be able to keep it inside anymore. I imagine that I'd blow up. Fact is that I'm not sure *what* I'd do."

"Is it possible," I said carefully, "that you're more afraid of *your* anger than his?"

She sat quietly for a moment, then smiled softly, and said, "Yes."

"Rage can be a totally disarming emotion," I said. "Is it possible that you stay with Jack because if he tried to stop you from leaving, you're not sure what *you* might do?"

"Absolutely."

Other LTL women may not be as explosive as Vivian, but their fear of anger keeps them silent until they over-react. This woman rages at her partner to stop his insensitive behavior. He, in turn, dismisses her anger as just so much female hysteria. The problem that originally concerned her is lost in the melee.

Women who are afraid of their anger make up a lot of excuses to cover their fear. "I don't want to upset the children" and "It won't help anything" are two self-explanations that supposedly rationalize not confronting one's partner.

This shortcoming flourishes in women with easy-going personalities. They are slow to panic, tolerant of others' peculiarities, patient, and thoughtful. These attributes are positive qualities—positive, that is, until the woman is treated with disrespect and she does nothing about it.

While fear of anger may be a part of a woman's nature, it's also the result of a culture that tells young females that "nice girls don't get angry." This misguided notion is usually reinforced by parents who somehow punish the girl if she outwardly shows her anger.

The LTL woman mistakenly believes that anger destroys love. The more she loves someone, the greater her fear that her anger would be destructive. Hence, her fear of anger is strongest with her partner (whom she loves the most), and weakest with a non-intimate stranger, for example, a checkout clerk (whom she loves the least).

This attitude creates a strange irony—*the deeper a woman's love, the greater her loneliness*. The chain reaction explaining this insight is as follows: as her love increases, so does her fear that anger will be destructive to that love; as her fear intensifies, she works harder to suppress her true feelings; the more she hides her feelings, the greater her sense of estrangement from her true self becomes; and, the more her estrangement grows, the deeper her feelings of emptiness inside and her loneliness become.

Lessons About Fear of Anger

- Fear of anger can cause a woman to endure an abusive relationship. Without constructive use of anger, an abused woman lacks the energy to escape the nightmare.

- You may fear anger because you believe that it will destroy your love. However, quite the opposite is true. Not expressing your anger and failing to get at its cause can create an estrangement that eventually *will* destroy love.

Narcissism

Narcissism is usually defined as an exaggerated belief in one's own power or importance. ''Macho man'' is an example of narcissism that comes immediately to mind. But women are also narcissistic. Take Jill, for example.

If you'll recall, Jill, the woman you met in chapter one, was thirty-nine, married to a successful salesman, had two children, and lived in relative affluence. She was college educated and worked as a legal assistant. She was the younger of two children, and though she tried her best to be an agreeable daughter, her mother was constantly critical of her.

Listen as Jill describes a classic example of female narcissism:

"I was fixing one meal for my kids," she said, "while preparing another for my husband, Paul. In between time, I tried to write a list for the PTA mothers' meeting so that other moms would know what to do on market day. I was on the phone trying to calm down my mother-in-law when Paul walked in and demanded to know who left the bike in the driveway. I tried to explain that the Johnson boy is poorly supervised and leaves his toys all over the neighborhood. Meanwhile, *my* mother called wanting to complain about my sister. Then, the kids started fighting. I'm afraid I lost it, and screamed at everybody. Paul looked at me like I was nuts."

When her children complained, Jill felt she was a bad mother. When her husband was critical, she felt she was a bad wife. In addition, she often felt she was a bad daughter, sister, and neighbor. Jill felt bad about herself so often because she *believed* that she could be all things to all people all of the time.

Jill had never learned how to take time for herself. When she tried to rest or "goofed off," she felt so guilty that she was forced to get busy on some project.

She equated taking time for herself with being selfish and lazy. Jill didn't know why she behaved this way, but recognized it as a lifelong habit.

Female narcissists believe that they have the power to cause other people to feel bad, that they can save a person from himself, and that their love can make other people change their actions. Needless to say, when they're not under pressure to perform a miracle, they're consumed with guilt over their latest failure.

Narcissists are often overachievers. They push themselves to excessive limits, expecting unrealistic recognition and reward. Here's the way Kelly, a thirty-one-year-old restaurant manager, described her overachievement.

"I worked hard in high school, always had a job, and was self-sufficient long before I went away to school. In college, I took a double major, had two summer jobs, and graduated with honors. But now, as a manager, I'm working harder than ever. I have to bring work home, I work on weekends, and still I never catch up. My husband and I spend all our money but never seem to enjoy it."

Overachievement kept Kelly in a permanent state of level-4 stress, a level that stress management professionals often refer to as, "the last step before burnout." Kelly was propelled by her own mental inertia, believing that she could solve any problem if only she threw enough work at it. However, she wasted time and energy while moving herself toward level-5 stress and eventual burnout.

Many narcissistic women push themselves to superhuman levels, all the while hoping to relieve their loneliness. But it only gets worse. Though on the verge of burnout and aching from loneliness, they still don't permit themselves to think about it. "It will go away," they tell themselves. When it doesn't, they just push it further from their minds. You can see why denial is a narcissist's best defense, and worst enemy.

A Lesson About Female Narcissism
• If you try to be everything to everyone, you'll end up being nothing to anyone, including yourself.

Powerlessness
When the LTL woman loses touch with her brain's power center, she loses the ability to take responsibility for her own life. Problem-solving is suspended as she reacts from habit, not from conscious thought. She no longer considers options, no longer sees herself as in charge of her own destiny. She permits her life to be run by chance, rather than by choice.

If you'll recall, I noted that my philosophy of Spiritual Behaviorism takes a person to the edge of her own self and encourages her to follow the principles of Truth, Hope, and Love in making the leap from the material to the spiritual. Powerlessness results when a person simply doesn't have the faith that he or she can make that leap.

Julie didn't have faith in herself. She was twenty-nine years old, college educated, attractive, and had a good job managing a jewelry store. Her relationship with her live-in partner, Keith, was on-again, off-again. They talked of getting married, but Julie resisted it.

Julie had a terrible time making up her own mind. Throughout her life, she seemed to simply *re*-act, permitting others to determine what she would do. At work, she allowed her subordinates to schedule their own workdays, and had a terrible time disciplining sloppy workers. The regional manager was beginning to question her competence.

At home, she reacted as if she were brainwashed. She went along with Keith, feeling powerless to make her thoughts known in a constructive manner.

"When Keith disagrees with me," Julie said, "I get confused and don't know what to say. I know that I should say something, but my mind seems to go blank."

"What happens?" I asked.

"I try to speak, he pressures me for my opinion, I usually say something stupid, and then he makes fun of me. The conversation dies right there."

"Does this happen all the time?"

"It seems to. It's getting to the point that I don't even want to try and talk anymore."

"Do you and Keith ever have any good times?" I said.

"Oh, sure," she said, "but only when we do something that he wants to do."

When confronted about her lack of responsibility, the powerless woman will say that she's hesitant to speak her mind because she doesn't want to become impulsive. She equates trusting oneself with being egotistical. She's lost sight of the balance between proper planning and spontaneity. At first glance, her powerlessness appears to be a fear of failure. But it's that and more. It's also a crisis of faith.

When I suggest to a powerless woman that she rekindle her self-faith and reactivate her power center, she goes to the opposite extreme, and hears me telling her to become narcissistic. However, the two are quite distinct, and can and do co-exist in the LTL woman.

When it comes to meeting other people's needs, the LTL woman is often narcissistic—she believes that she can, and must, meet those needs. But, when it comes to meeting her own needs, she feels helpless. She feels responsible for creating a situation, but feels powerless to do anything about it.

Lessons About Powerlessness

- If you feel powerless, you believe that you can't do anything about your loneliness. You're wrong. Your brain/soul connection will give you the knowledge and energy that's necessary to overcome the feeling.

- Feelings of powerlessness are often accompanied by feelings of foolishness, similar to the ones we all experienced during adolescence. If certain situations make you feel as if you're forty going on fourteen, you may be experiencing powerlessness, and you need to take more action in those situations.

There's considerable overlap and interplay among the four shortcomings. Your low self-esteem can cause you to invalidate your anger, to blame yourself for causing all the problems around you, and to convince yourself of your powerlessness to solve any problems. Fear of anger can rob you of the energy to confront frightening issues, making you feel even more powerless. Your feeling of impotence can push you to be all things to all people, leaving you no time or energy to nurture your self-esteem.

ROLE CONFLICT: OLD RULES AND NEW EXPECTATIONS

The old rules dictated that femininity was synonymous with subservience. Being coupled with a man was acceptable, living by yourself was not; expecting a man to support you was the norm, being a career woman was the exception; a man's opinion was dominant, a woman's insignificant.

Despite the changes, the old rules are still very much alive. They are part of nearly every woman's early childhood conditioning. Even the "liberated" woman has a tendency to use the old rules, especially when she has the personality shortcomings mentioned above.

The new expectations spell out a new attitude. Expect more out of your life, be independent, and think for yourself. Most importantly, they tell a woman to expect direct, rather than indirect, satisfaction from life, especially regarding intimacy from her partner.

But what is it, exactly, that she's supposed to do? "Expect respect"—but what does that mean? "Put yourself first"—but isn't that being selfish? "Your opinion counts"—but can't that lead to being overbearing? The problem with the new expectations is that *they don't spell out new rules* (and this is the norm during any cultural transition, at least in a democratic society).

When the old rules clash with the new expectations, the result is a role conflict. Your brain's power center is put into a double bind, pushed by its nature to attain the freedom and dignity of the new expectations, yet pulled by uncertainty and tradition to remain silent. This bind stimulates even more anxiety.

High anxiety, typically, causes a person to take action from habit rather than from willful purpose. Hence, it allows the old rules to often win out, and because you have put your power center on hold, you automatically do what you've always done. However, the brain/soul connection cannot be silenced, and it says, in effect, "There you go again, doing the same old, self-defeating thing!"

I have two pragmatic reasons for suggesting that you take the path toward new expectations. First, if you persist in using the old rules to cope with your situation, your anxiety will lead you in circles, and your loneliness will worsen. Second, the anxiety you'll suffer in exploring the new expectations will be worth the hassle, eventually leading you to a new, more effective way of living.

Below, I've examined a few of the old rules that are used by LTL women when attempting to cope with their anxiety. In each case, I've included a new expectation that conflicts with that rule.

As you read each of these, try to determine which ones bog you down the most in your everyday life. If you can pinpoint those "buttons" of yours that are easily pushed, it will help you later on in creating your path toward wholeness.

Old Rule One: Exercise control over a loved one, and you'll have belonging.

Danielle, a thirty-two-year-old systems' analyst, was a woman overwhelmed with feelings of powerlessness.

She sought to overcome her distress by controlling her husband, Casey. Instead of finding power, she became the target of Casey's manipulation. She tolerated it because she really thought that she was controlling him, as well as herself. In truth, neither Danielle nor Casey demonstrated any self-control.

When your man asks your permission to go hunting, fishing, or out with the boys, he's casting you in the role of his mother. As he did with her, he then tries to manipulate you into approving of his plans so that he won't get nervous about your getting angry. If you adhere to Old Rule One, you'll argue with him, try to make him feel guilty, or otherwise look for a way to control him. In the end, your control procedures will fail and you'll go along with his manipulation.

This rule was supposed to protect you from getting hurt, but instead, it resulted in alienation, cynicism, and suspicion, three of the building blocks of loneliness.

New Expectation: You are only responsible for yourself.

Old Rule Two: Expect and tolerate insensitivity from a loved one.

Iris, fifty, had been married to Ernie for twenty-five years. Ernie wasn't a bad guy, but he was abrupt and ill-mannered. Iris had been conditioned in the love/punishment connection by parents who'd say, "I'm only punishing you because I love you." They did not show their "love" at other times. Not surprisingly, Iris began tolerating Ernie's insensitivity soon after they started dating. She never stopped.

Adherents to Old Rule Two make excuses for their

man's insensitivity, drive themselves goofy trying to make him see the error of his ways, or simply endure his rancor because they believe that they, themselves, might be wrong. These are the women who, after I've pointed out examples of his continued emotional abuse, dismiss the entire situation by saying, "But I love him." These are also the women who, when encountering a kind and decent man, become suspicious of his motives.

Old-Rule-Two conformists are prime candidates for developing crippling bitterness. By tolerating insensitivity, not only do they continually deny their soul the nurturance it so desperately needs, but also they dump frustration and pessimism on their otherwise-optimistic human spirit.

New Expectation: Expect respect.

Old Rule Three: One person should analyze a two-person problem.

Abby, the counselor-in-training you met earlier, was especially vulnerable to this rule. As a well-read, psychologically sophisticated woman, she implemented this rule immediately after experiencing an isolating behavior from her husband, Justin. "If I can figure out why he's doing this," she'd say, "I can resolve it." Abby's low self-esteem and tendency toward narcissism caused her to believe that she had superhuman powers.

This rule permits your man, parent, sibling, or child to use you as a "whipping girl." Your man belittles you, and you're so consumed with assessing *his* insecurity that you don't confront him. Your mother blasts you for not paying enough attention to her, and you're frozen by your compulsion to figure out why she's treating you so badly. As a result, you say nothing and feel empty inside.

Your older sister makes a snide remark about your new car, and you swallow it, too busy analyzing her jealousy to tell her to quit being nasty. Your teenage son snaps at you and, rather than warning him about his disrespect, you are immobilized by your excessive concern about his adolescent identity crisis.

It's fine to analyze interpersonal problems and try to figure out the best solution. Fine, that is, if *both* of you are working at the solution. Otherwise, your analysis actually helps you avoid confronting the problem as it further isolates you.

New Expectation: People should solve problems together.

Old Rule Four: Give unconditionally and you'll avoid rejection.

This rule is most active in those whose low self-esteem dominates their other personality flaws. It's triggered whenever fear of rejection surfaces. The central erroneous element in this rule is the belief that a person can keep giving adult love without getting any in return. The fact is that, without nurturance, adult love dies.

Pat, a thirty-three-year-old mother of two, gave to everyone and rarely, if ever, got anything in return. She was always there when her husband complained about his work, but he didn't listen to her complaints. When one of her sisters got sick, she was the first one to bring food and to offer to watch her children. But everyone seemed to disappear when she needed help. Though it was Pat who listened to her mother's incessant gripes, it was her uncaring sister who received Mom's special gifts.

The *unconditional giver* drives herself into isolation by serving up gourmet meals to a chronically critical partner, by running errands for an unappreciative spouse, or by always listening to his complaints without expecting him to return the courtesy.

New Expectation: Sometimes, your needs come first.

Old Rule Five: Behaving perfectly is another way to find belonging.

Harriet was a lifelong advocate of this rule. The forty-seven-year-old schoolteacher treated her husband, George, like a king and herself as his servant. Everything she did had to be done perfectly or else she was upset with herself. If George, who really wasn't a bad sort, made a slightly critical remark about a meal or noticed dirt on the floor, Harriet couldn't rest until she fixed different food or polished the linoleum.

Harriet wasn't aware that she was largely responsible for her own loneliness. She believed, as so many LTL women do, that the key to overcoming loneliness is to gain other people's approval, especially her husband's. "Once people approve of me," she thought to herself, "my emptiness will cease and I'll belong."

This dyslogia forces a woman to assess a situation as quickly as possible, figure out who the dominant persons are and how to please them, and then perform the prescribed role as perfectly as possible. The rule does not allow for the expression of one's individuality, and the power center suffers from disuse. The criticism of another person, whether it's constructive or not, is anathema.

Most perfectionistic women honestly don't realize that their goals are unrealistic. Their narcissism drives them to perfection, while their powerlessness makes it nearly impossible for them to stop the treadmill. Once they try to be perfect, they can never be perfect enough.

New Expectation: You have the right to be wrong.

Old Rule Six: To avoid feeling lonely, avoid self-disclosure.

When I first challenged Harriet to harness her brain's power center and to renew her faith in herself, she hit me with the "Yes, but . . ." defense. "Yes, I see your point, Dr. Kiley," she said, "but I couldn't possibly say that." She remained steadfast in the face of continued pressure. "Yes, I understand your suggestion, but George would never go along with it."

The main strategy of Harriet's "Yes, but . . ." defense was to protect her fragile self-esteem from the vulnerability inherent in self-disclosure—the act of confiding in another. She didn't realize that camouflaging her inner self and denying her power center and Truth actually increased her resentment and uncertainty, forcing more distance between her and George. The greater the distance between them, the more intense Harriet's LTL experience became.

In his book *The Transparent Self*, Dr. Sidney Jourard calls self-disclosure "the portal to a person's soul." Though she may mouth words to the contrary, an LTL woman often doesn't want her partner to see her soul.

She doesn't trust him with such a precious gift, fearing that if he sees her true inner self, he may reject it.

As she protects herself from loneliness by avoiding self-disclosure, the LTL woman begins to lose touch with herself, her power center, and her Truth. Alienation from her partner leads to alienation from herself. In the end, she falls deeper into the very thing she's trying to avoid—loneliness.

New Expectation: You deserve to be loved just the way you are.

Old Rule Seven: Maintaining peace-at-any-price will turn away anger and create a sense of self-control.

Thirty-seven-year-old Linda, an energetic woman with dazzling eyes and a refined sense of elegance, had been taught the peacemaker role early in life.

"Back away, placate, do whatever you must, but maintain peace, no matter what the price." This was the self-instruction she'd recited to herself during her early years. Her dominant shortcomings were her feelings of powerlessness and a fear of her own anger. She adhered to the childhood conditioning that told her anger was bad. Consequently, she avoided expressing her anger, and therefore she never learned how to use it constructively.

"I grew up as the peacemaker in my family. I was the one who did the dishes when my mom yelled at my sister. I cleaned up after my little brother so that he wouldn't get into trouble. Mom and Dad, even my teachers, all used to point to me as the example of a 'good girl.'

"I took a course in group dynamics at college. We

used to analyze the roles we played in various situations. The other students always identified me as the 'ameliorator,' the one who tried to smooth things out so that there were no hassles.''

Trying to ''smooth things out'' can be an admirable trait, but it can get out of hand.

The main strategy of the ''peacemaker'' is found in this corollary to Old Rule Seven: *No matter what the criticism, an explanation is in order.* Linda became defensive in the face of her husband, Jimmy's, excessive criticisms. When he made a sarcastic comment about leftovers for dinner, Linda gave him a step-by-step explanation of why she was late and couldn't make dinner. When he made fun of her new hairstyle, she went to great lengths to explain why she'd had it done and how it would grow out quickly. She couldn't confront him, or just walk away, because Jimmy might get mad and the uproar would violate the peacemaker rule.

The LTL woman utilizes this rule with people other than her partner. She finds herself going along with a demanding parent even though she'll hate herself later. She loses herself in justifying her parental actions to a manipulative teenager. She even gets defensive when a neighbor whom she doesn't like makes a snide comment about her windows being dirty. She's prisoner to a rule that's supposed to give her belonging, but only increases her loneliness.

New Expectation: You have a right to get angry.

Old Rule Eight: When facing isolation and anxiety, acquire possessions, and the ''right'' friends.

Meet Jackie, a forty-four-year-old woman married to Dave, also forty-four. They have two children, a cat, and a boat. Dave is a real estate broker, Jackie a trained social worker who volunteers her time at a shelter for battered women.

On the surface, Jackie appeared happy. As the daughter of a prominent community leader, her childhood had been one of affluence and privilege. She'd attended the finest schools and married a man destined to be a leader of society. She had everything a woman might want, her own Mercedes, a thirty-foot sailboat, and a lovely home near the golf course. She also had a severe case of LTL.

As a child, Jackie learned that love is a tool of barter. Her parents used the phrase, "If you love me, you'll do as I ask" to pressure her into complying with their wishes, be it to eat more vegetables, or to date the son of a doctor. They further controlled her behavior by bribing her with money and possessions when she did as they wanted. As an adult, Jackie tried to buy her way out of loneliness. It didn't work.

Although I was clearly indifferent to talk of her shopping habits, Jackie seemed unable to stop telling me about shopping at Tiffany's, vacationing on the French Riviera, and wearing Albert Nipon dresses. Since she'd been taught that love had a price tag on it, she naturally, when her anxiety and fear of rejection surfaced, tried to buy love and acceptance.

Jackie was also the victim of adult peer pressure. She immersed herself in a mad dash for sameness, working tirelessly to keep company with people that she wanted to emulate. She kept so busy entertaining the "right" people, and espousing the "correct" causes, that she didn't have the time or the energy to confront the absence of warmth and empathy in her relationship.

New Expectation: Being alone is okay.

Old Rule Nine: When the anxiety becomes too great, search for a simpler answer.

Women who follow this rule turn away from the complicated issues involved in LTL, and try to find an easier solution. They make the mistake of "reductionism." That is, they reduce a problem down to such a simple level that they lose touch with it. One could argue that reductionism is a form of denial (see Old Rule Ten).

Sherril was thirty-six, divorced, and currently living with forty-seven-year-old Johnny. They were planning to marry as soon as Johnny received his divorce. Though she and Johnny said all the right words about commitment, their relationship was stilted and unemotional.

When I asked Sherril about her hopes for her married life, she began lecturing me about the fount of true knowledge, the transcendental nature of love, and ontological insecurity. Taken aback, I asked her what she was talking about. She told me that it was metaphysics, something that I should look into. She tried to convince me that her gibberish was part of her spiritual life, but her words were neither life-like nor reflective of inner faith and contentment.

While Sherril hid in metaphysics, Lisa, a twenty-five-year-old, college-educated researcher for the federal government, found her refuge in religiosity.

Six months after getting married, Lisa was bewildered. She'd thought that Jeff, her husband, believed in women's rights. Instead, he turned out to be a dyed-in-the-wool chauvinist, expecting her to meet his every need without reciprocation. As her loneliness deepened, Lisa went to the extreme in expecting an organized religion to relieve her feelings of emptiness.

Lisa recited scripture in explaining away Jeff's chauvinistic attitudes, quoted religious dogma when asked why she'd made certain personal decisions. Also, she reduced every controversial issue down to a rigid, black-and-white interpretation, thus inhibiting any discussion. (A distinction should be made between religiosity, a rote, superficial practice, and true religiousness, which has a spiritual underpinning.)

Because religion is the "great connector"—it provides many people with a bridge to others—it can be an effective tonic for lonesomeness, the type of loneliness that we all experience from time to time. Nurturing your own spirituality gives you a sense of internal enlightenment, rather like plugging in a string of lights at Christmastime. The darkness of lonesomeness is lifted by the promise that there's meaning beyond this lonely moment.

Lisa found some relief from loneliness in her religious beliefs. Unfortunately, she expected her religion to solve LTL just as it can solve lonesomeness. But it would never work, because there are psychological aspects to LTL that religion, by itself, cannot solve. By making unrealistic demands upon a system of spirituality, and by taking a powerful source of comfort to an extreme, Lisa robbed herself of her self-control and her loneliness worsened.

Lisa had sought my help regarding a career decision.

When I suggested that she might be *Living Together, Feeling Alone*, she pointedly disagreed, asked to terminate the session, and walked out. She did not return.

Both metaphysics and religiosity have the same glowing defect: They try to *implant* spirituality from the outside rather than nurturing it from the inside. Women who use these two methods to implement Old Rule Nine don't realize that they are running away from an old pain, not discovering a new Truth.

New Expectation: You have a right to be anxious and confused.

Old Rule Ten: When all else fails, push the conflict and confusion out of your mind.

Those of you familiar with Margaret Mitchell's *Gone With the Wind* will recognize the character of Scarlett O'Hara and her procrastination. When faced with a problem, Scarlett dismisses it by saying that she'll think about it all tomorrow. Unfortunately, tomorrow only brings more procrastination.

Denial is the simplest, yet most dangerous, tactic of all. It allows you to push the things out of your mind that you don't wish to think about. Several years ago I worked with Ronnie, a forty-four-year-old woman who had a charming personality and three marvelous children. Her marriage to Cliff, however, was an empty shell. Though she sought my help for her marriage, she steadfastly denied her loneliness. She also denied the seriousness of alarming physical symptoms. By the time she went to a physician, her uterine cancer had become inoperable.

Yet denial is not all bad. There are situations in

which it can work in your favor. For example, after you've gotten at least two opinions about a serious surgery, and selected the best surgeon and hospital, research suggests that people who deny a long recuperative period ("I'll be up and around in no time"), actually get better more quickly than do people who continually mull over the side effects of physical limitations. The difference between "good" and "bad" denial is this: Denial can be good *provided* that you do everything possible about the problem before pushing it out of your mind.

New Expectation: Your opinions count.

You'll probably see yourself caught in at least one of these conflicts. Don't bother adding up your rule infractions or trying to give yourself an anxiety score. It's enough that you recognize the role conflicts that are a part of your daily life. Now, it's time to identify the symptoms and then begin your treatment.

5

Symptoms of LTL

By now you have some sense that your dormant power center is alive and well after all. Your LTL has been validated—it's real, not imagined—and your relationship to society, your mate, and yourself can be seen in terms of some preconceived and often erroneous expectations. While allowing some painful denied truths to rise to the forefront of your mind, let's examine how ten different women appear to the outside world. Remember, in order to love yourself, you have to be honest with yourself.

Nine of the ten symptoms to be discussed in this chapter, with the exception of bitterness and blame, can be considered problems in and of themselves. For example, substance abuse, sexual promiscuity, and depression all have behavior patterns that are directly observable. One can look at the behavior and say, "Yes, that's depression," or "That's substance abuse."

Because of its spiritual component, loneliness does not afford that clarity. What you see is not necessarily what you get. You can look at sexual promiscuity and not see loneliness. Often, promiscuity can be exactly what it appears to be—the flagrant disregard of sexual moral values—nothing more.

How is one to tell, therefore, when a problem behavior is self-contained, and when it's a symptom of loneliness? The answer lies in studying case histories and engaging in a process known as *differentiation*.

Differentiation occurs as you answer the question, "In what ways am I different from people with whom I identify?" Differentiation will lead to insight because, as you read about these women's experiences and my explanations, you'll compare and contrast your life to their lives and learn to identify *how* your life is *different*. By examining ten symptoms of loneliness, you'll gradually understand how loneliness *uniquely* manifests itself in your life. Once you've done that, you'll be better prepared to deal with it.

BITTERNESS AND BLAME

Cynicism and contempt dramatically increase when a woman lives with a man in what was expected to be a loving relationship but, in fact, is characterized by ostracism and isolation. There's a clear relationship between the length of time a woman feels she's been *Living Together, Feeling Alone* and the degree of bitterness felt and where or at whom blame is directed. The Bewildered woman's bitterness is not yet focused on her man, while the Isolated woman expresses sarcastic disapproval for the way *her* particular man treats her. Cynicism and contempt for men *in general* hit a peak during the Agitation stage and remain fairly constant throughout the Depression stage. Bitterness takes its toll on a woman in the Exhausted stage; the pain of too many years of wasted hope and too many days of disappointment saps her energy and blunts her ability to care.

Whenever bitterness exists, blame—the attribution of fault to someone because of a misdeed—is sure to follow. The LTL woman seeks to ease her bitterness by blaming her man for her pain. She believes that blame will result in his shame, and that shame will motivate him to mend his ways. When he doesn't change, her bitterness intensifies, as does her blaming.

Eventually, shame backfires on the blame-thrower. The shame-ridden partner rebels against blame, seeking revenge. He'll blame you for his shame and do something to make himself feel better.

Bitterness consumes massive amounts of psychic energy without returning any strength to the body or soul. Bitterness takes, it doesn't give. The only consistent effect of bitterness is that it slowly devours the embittered person.

I believe that bitterness is the mechanism that makes LTL a killer. The stress of bitterness suppresses the body's immune system, leaving the person vulnerable to a variety of invading diseases. I've found that bitterness and blame are two symptoms shared by nearly all LTL women.

When I asked forty-one-year-old Sylvia why she'd come to see me, she began sharing her married problems. The more the perky grocery clerk talked about her husband, Sidney, the more excited and hostile she became. After working her way through a litany of his offenses, Sylvia looked me squarely in the eyes and, assuming that I wouldn't take it personally, said, "All men are bastards!"

When she wasn't blasting away at the male of the species, Sylvia was a delightfully engaging woman. She wanted to become a beautician, and made no apologies for the fact that she was using herself as a cosmetological guinea pig. On our first visit, her hair was coal black with a three-inch-wide, blood-red streak running from above her left eye over her head to her right ear. She called it her vampire look. When she bared her teeth in bitterness, the title was all too real.

Although she didn't see it, Sylvia's bitterness had been born long before her marriage. As a child, she'd been spanked frequently, for offenses ranging from teasing the cat to spilling milk. She'd learned to expect physical punishment for behaviors that just didn't justify such measures.

Early in her high school years, the spankings turned from physical to emotional. When Sylvia experimented with flirtatious behavior, she was labeled "that kind of girl." A close friendship with a female cousin brought the reminder from her mom that there was homosexuality in the family. When she was assertive, she was called aggressive; when she was silent, she was accused of being ill-mannered.

What made these abusive tactics so much more damaging was the fact that they'd occurred at approximately the same time that she'd been told that she was loved. The words were of love, but their actions were of punishment.

The result was that Sylvia became conditioned to expect and tolerate punishing behavior from those whom she loved. Not surprisingly, she carried a perpetual chip on her shoulder, looking for places to dump her frustration. Sidney gave her plenty of chances.

"The other day," she said, explaining one of her outbursts, "Sidney told me about a problem he was having with his co-workers. 'I don't know what to do about it,' he said. I told him that he should treat his co-worker the way he treats me, like dirt. 'Give him heartburn,' I said. 'That'll make me feel like I'm not alone.' I went after him for ten or fifteen minutes. I'm not proud of it, but it gave me a feeling of revenge."

Sylvia's bitterness hurt her self-esteem. She couldn't help but look in the mirror and see a jaded, unhappy person. She really wasn't a cruel person, but she was caught in a punishment cycle. When people were nice to her, she was confused and uncertain. But when they were punishing, she felt grounded in reality, almost comfortable. She'd married Sidney because his insensitivity rang a bell of familiarity. She knew how to act. Love and punishment had made horrible bedfellows in her life.

If bitterness has a hold on your brain and soul, don't condemn yourself. Take it as evidence that you need to redirect some of the energies in your life. It makes little difference whether your man is a Dr. Jekyll or a Mr. Hyde. You need an understanding of *your* personality shortcoming and role conflicts so that you know where your problems end and his begin.

Lessons About Bitterness/Blame

- Solving a problem is the best antidote for bitterness. You can't solve a problem if you blame another person for your feelings.

• Make a distinction between blaming your partner and holding him responsible for his behavior.

If you blame him, you're saying, in effect, "you are controlling my feelings and I can't feel better unless you change." If you hold him responsible for his behavior, then you're saying, "Unless you become more loving, I'll have to do something to reduce my isolation."

In the former, you lose control over your life. In the latter, you have a wide range of options given the nature of the situation. Your choice may range from going to a movie while he's watching football, to seeking advice from a marriage counselor.

If your man sees your warning as a threat, remind him that *his* behavior is a threat to your relationship; your behavior is an attempt to save the relationship.

• It bears repeating: Blaming your man makes it practically impossible for you to change your situation. *Your man does not cause your loneliness.*

WEIGHT PROBLEMS

Our culture tells all of us, especially women, that "thin is in." Being thin will bring romance, excitement, a whole new life. Fat will keep you trapped in the doldrums, and make you unacceptable. Thin promises recognition and belonging. If you're thin, you won't be lonely.

Many an LTL woman is constantly battling her weight. Few recognize that, in waging war on fat, she is, in fact, waging war on her own self-esteem. Her thoughts may run something like this: "I'm fat and therefore, unacceptable as a person. If I were thin, I'd be a better person and other people would like me."

This terribly destructive attitude comes from a low self-esteem. When this kind of negative self-referencing motivates the weight reduction scheme, failure is inevitable. The cycle of self-deprecation/failed diet/self-deprecation begins again. It's unrealistic to expect yourself to follow through on a sensible dietary program when you're constantly belittling your soul.

Despite the mythology surrounding the glory of thinness, human beings can't live without fat. Even the health fanatics tell us that having some fat is good. As a woman, it's perfectly acceptable to have about 18 to 25 percent of your body weight in fat, depending on your age.

There seems to be a cultural conspiracy that says, if you have, say, twenty pounds of body fat, you're a marvelous lover, a fantastic sex object, and a perfect fit for the new fall line of clothes. But, add a few more pounds of that same substance, and poof! you're now an inadequate, unloved person, who's destined for loneliness. Obviously, the fat/self-esteem connection is irrational and should be replaced with thinking to ourselves, "I'm a perfectly acceptable human being, who just happens to be carrying around twenty-five pounds of unneeded tissue." When a negative self-reference is exchanged for a positive self-reference, you have finally gotten the fat out of your mind, and can now go to work on the fat on your stomachs and hips.

Thirty-eight-year-old Annie was about fifty pounds overweight. She'd quit her job as a legal secretary, to start her own office-cleaning business because of her fat/self-esteem connection. Having to dress up every day and have every little detail of her appearance scrutinized by the "Brook's Brothers' Brigade" had become too stressful.

Ironically, her first office-cleaning job was for her previous employer. "I walked in there," she said, "looked around, and saw things I'd never seen before. The carpet was gray, the walls were gray, the furniture was gray, even the plants were gray. I realized that the people had been gray, and even I'd become gray."

It took Annie several weeks before she could talk openly about her weight-control problem. Once the subject was open, insecurity literally poured out from her soul. She'd been to physicians, weight-control clinics, and had tried every diet under the sun. "I stay on the diet for a week or two, lose a few pounds, and then something happens and I'm back at the refrigerator. I'm obsessed with food."

I countered Annie's negativism by reminding her that she might be "obsessed" with giving and receiving love rather than with food. Many people who say that they're obsessed with food are actually trying to cope with loneliness by recreating the feelings of love and belonging that existed during childhood mealtime. In these cases, eating is strongly associated with belonging. When a person feels as if she doesn't belong, she craves love and attention, and food is the symbol.

If you're overweight and feel obsessed with food, don't be so quick to condemn yourself. Repeat the positive self-reference from above, and remember that your desire for food may, in fact, simply be a misdirected attempt to escape your loneliness.

Lessons to Learn About Weight Problems
• Weight-loss problems have a strong correlation with low self-esteem and powerlessness. Be aware that food is only a temporary cure for loneliness.

SUBSTANCE ABUSE

It's estimated that there are 18 million problem drinkers in the United States. If abusers of other controlled substances, including prescription drugs, are added to this figure, the number easily exceeds 10 percent of the population.

Research suggests that 20 to 30 percent of these substance abusers are women. My experience takes that statistic one step further. Of the LTL women that I've studied in depth, 34 percent had some problem with alcohol and 22 percent admitted to taking more than the prescribed number of tranquilizers (there was some overlap between these two groups).

Dr. Sharon Wilsnack of the North Dakota School of Medicine, discovered that older women who identify primarily with feminine traits (nurturance, passivity, dependence) were at a high risk for alcoholism. At low risk were women who could be both strong and assertive, and warm and loving—women who were in touch with and trusted their power centers.

It's not enough, however, to say that LTL women abuse controlled substances because they follow the old rules of femininity. There are other causes, such as numbing the pain of loneliness, freeing one's sexual inhibitions, responding to a genetic tendency toward alcoholism, or seeing alcohol or a drug as a reliable old friend.

Alison had worked hard to perfect the image of a woman in control. The forty-three-year-old housewife had a marvelous vocabulary, was soft-spoken, and well-read. Her forty-five-year-old husband, Hunter, had been a professional basketball player, and remained active in his college alumni organization.

At first, all Alison wanted to do was complain about Hunter and tell me what *his* problems were. When I tried to get her to focus on *her* feelings, she was vague and denied her part in the couples' problems. She hid her feelings so successfully she didn't even know what they were. It took several weeks before I was able to get Alison to admit that she was a substance abuser. She drank at least two cocktails or glasses of wine every night, seven days a week. She was addicted to tranquilizers, took sleeping pills several nights a week, and sometimes had a glass of vodka with lunch.

Hunter had a great deal of his own self-esteem invested in his appearance as a happy man with a trouble-free marriage. He found it exceedingly difficult to admit that substance abuse was destroying his family, and that he was nearly as dependent upon alcohol and drugs as Alison.

When I asked him if Alison drank too much, he was uncomfortable and evasive. "Yes, No, Maybe, I don't know." After continued pressure, I discovered that he avoided confronting Alison about her drinking, preferring to make indirect and subtle remarks about reducing consumption. He would drink with her in an attempt to slow down her consumption. He tried to distract her from her "cocktail hour." He mixed her drinks for her, using less liquor. In short, he hid from the reality of her substance abuse just as much as she did, *and* he organized a good deal of his life to accommodate it. This made him codependent.

LTL substance abusers are often adult children of alcoholics. If they accept and understand the impact of their childhood experiences, it's easier for them to accept and to understand their own addiction.

I asked Alison to read a book on adult children of alcoholics. She returned a week later with the first glimpse of insight. "I think that my mother took her frustration out on me," she said. "Her life was run by alcohol just as much as my father's. In fact, *my* life was run by liquor. The whole family was alcoholic."

When I pushed her toward the awareness that her life was *still* run by liquor, she was slow to agree. "After what I went through as a child," she said, "do you think I could let myself fall into the same trap?"

"Yes," I said gently. "Because you never took control of your life away from liquor."

A Lesson About Substance Abuse
• The good feeling that results from substance abuse is a lie.

DEPRESSION

The National Institute of Mental Health says that depression afflicts 10 million people, twice as many women as men. Among the major symptoms of depression are: disturbances of eating and/or sleeping, sexual indifference, withdrawal from previously enjoyable activities, continuous feelings of gloom and doom, thoughts of suicide, mood swings, and crying spells. A person doesn't have to have all of these symptoms to be depressed.

As you already know, I've found that some women who are diagnosed as depressed are, instead, suffering from LTL. There's no doubt that these women are depressed, but I believe that may not be their *main* problem. If they receive treatment only for their depression, and their loneliness is ignored or otherwise invalidated, their treatment, including the use of prescription drugs, will mask, not solve, their problem.

At first glance, forty-two-year-old Marsha appeared to be depressed, not lonely. When she wasn't sleeping, she sat around and did nothing, she told me. Her job performance was deteriorating, as was her concern for her marriage. She had abandoned tasks she once found enjoyable such as housekeeping, jogging, and talking with her friends. She felt as if life had nothing to offer her.

While there was no doubt that Marsha was depressed, it was important to determine if this was her *primary* problem. It could have been secondary to loneliness. The course of treatment would depend upon an accurate diagnosis.

Her depression scores on the survey of feelings were elevated but not as high as her symptoms suggested they might have been. Furthermore, the clear dominance of bewildered feelings was consistent with those of a relatively newly married woman (Marsha was married less than two years at the time). Also, clinically depressed people usually feel more isolated and exhausted than Marsha did.

After a lengthy, in-depth interview, I found three more pieces of information that convinced me Marsha's depression was masking LTL. First, though she ignored her own home, she happily cleaned her mother's house once a week. It didn't make sense that she'd withdraw from cleaning in such a selective way. Second, each of her complaints about her job, education, and financial status somehow related back to her dissatisfaction with her marriage. Finally, her fantasy about her husband, Mike, dying in a car accident was more characteristic of loneliness than of depression.

Marsha's depression was an indirect way of coping with the emptiness of her relationship. Her unkempt home and job deterioration were her way of digging in her heels, much as a four-year-old might do, and saying, "I'm going to hold my breath till I turn blue and then you'll be sorry."

Once she accepted this interpretation and practiced more direct confrontation of Mike's behavior, her depressive symptoms abated. She attributed this change to the validation of her loneliness, and to the realization that she was hurting herself more than Mike. Her reaction confirmed that loneliness, not depression, was her major problem.

LTL depression usually reflects a woman's inability to make the leap from the material to the spiritual world. Her brain's power center is malfunctioning and her self-faith is weakened from years of neglect. Thus, when she tries to implement change, she gets bogged down in role conflicts, disorder, and the other chaos that exists when one is unable to close the gap between expectations and reality.

Many LTL women who are depressed are strong proponents of Old Rule Seven (Peacemaking turns away anger and leads to self-control). They typically have a history of being the family ameliorator. They have sublimated their own needs and desires to the "greater good" so often that they lose sight of their own truth, and their power center becomes a dim memory. As children, they tried to keep their siblings out of trouble, and to please their parents and other adults at any cost. As adults, they continue to do whatever it takes to keep everyone happy. Everyone, that is, but themselves.

Marsha's peacemaking attitudes developed during childhood, but didn't cause her any significant trouble until she married. Now, peace-at-any-price was turning her into a zombie. She muted her feelings, silenced her power center (which urged her to take a stand for herself), and crushed her self-faith. She may have been able to generate peace on the outside, but there was a war going on within her.

If you're suffering from moderate depression, you may think it means that you've given up. People with severe depression often do. But you, like most LTL women, have a lot of fight left in you. If you're a peacemaker, doesn't it make sense for you to have fought back in a quiet, peaceful way? But, if you've done so, your depression could now be anger turned inward (where it hurts only you), instead of outward (where it might hurt others and thus violate your peace-at-any-price belief).

Lessons About Peacemaking and Depression

• The peacemaker's depression can be a way of resisting further sacrifice. If you want more peace in your life, you'll never get it by hiding your feelings.

Change can come only when you activate your power center and increase your self-faith.

• Even assertive women are not immune to the peace-making philosophy. Just because you were able to confront him during your cohabitation does *not* mean that you'll automatically be able to do it after you're married. The long-term commitment of marriage changes your expectations, making your interactions more serious.

• If you're a peacemaker, you must distinguish between times when going along to get along is good, and situations in which it's time to take a stand. For example, it's inappropriate if your man is always defining what kind of "fun" the two of you will have. Once in a while, you need to suggest a movie, play, or something else that *you* enjoy.

ANXIETY

Anxiety is like a dense cloud of smoke engulfing your brain and soul. It drains strength from your power center, forcing you to rely on old habits rather than pursuing new expectations. It distorts your vision of the future, making it relatively easy for you to fall into the abyss of depression. Finally, it robs your soul of the clarity provided by an increase in faith.

Anxiety can cause you to think of two opposing thoughts at the same time, and believe they will somehow make sense. They don't, of course, and soon you're looking in the mirror, wondering which end is up. Your confidence in meeting life's challenges is weakened, and you fall back into your old, ineffective ways. Anxiety is a monster that feeds on itself.

Elaine's anxiety made her a nervous wreck. She was forty-five and married to Harve, also forty-five. They had one child, a thirteen-year-old daughter. Harve was a banker, and Elaine, a Yale Law School graduate, worked a few hours a week as a tax lawyer.

Though Elaine tried to hide from her loneliness, her contradictory thoughts gave her away.

She denied any bitterness, then two minutes later said, "If I put as much time into myself as I have into Harve, I'd be the President of Chrysler Corporation." Her infectious smile melted into tears.

Her Bewilderment category score was low (9), yet she said, "I'm getting more from my husband than I ever imagined possible, but I've never been more dissatisfied." She initially denied any feelings of being unloved or abandoned, yet said, "If we make love once a year, it's a miracle." She scoffed at the idea that she felt "broken" or "numb," but said later, "I got trapped when I was thirteen and never escaped."

When I asked her to rate her anger, she said, "Oh, that's a 10." She paused briefly, then added, "I have to learn to get over my anger. I keep ruminating on twenty-three years of mistakes, and I'm turning into a bitch. I deserve the anger." She tried desperately to maintain her composure, but was on the verge of sobbing.

She scored sadness as a 10, but denied being depressed. Thirty minutes later, when I asked about feelings of worthlessness, she snapped, "I shouldn't have to put up with feeling so badly." Although Elaine's anxiety was very high and her depression very real, both of these elements were secondary to her fundamental problem—she was lonely.

Elaine had been raised in an atmosphere of bartered love by cold, aloof parents. She had also been victimized by the painful words of conditional love, "You'd do it if you loved me."

In a concerted effort to reduce her anxiety, Elaine had mastered nearly all of the old rules early in her life. She was exceptionally skilled at perfect behavior (Old Rule Five) and peace-at-any-price (Old Rule Seven). The conflict between the old rules and new expectations was especially difficult for her. Each time she tried to take control of her own life, rejection reared its ugly head and her anxiety skyrocketed.

Elaine's loneliness was complicated by the disparity between her emotional and chronological ages. Intellectually and physically, she was a mature woman; her feelings, however, were those of a fourteen-year-old. Because loneliness is most lethal during adolescence (contrary to popular opinion, loneliness does not hit its peak during old age), Elaine was not only *Living Together, Feeling Alone* but, in a way, she was doing it as a lonely teenager.

Lessons About Anxiety

• Affluence presents a temptation for parents to give material goods to their children instead of time and attention. If we attempt to secure belonging the same way we achieved physical security—that is, by purchasing it—we will, in fact, isolate ourselves even further.

• Many LTL women lack confidence in giving and receiving love. Their behavior often resembles that of a girl in her early to mid-adolescence. Love has become a weekly allowance, dispensed at the whim and will of another. Understandably, they rebel. If you're in love but resisting that love, or if loving makes you anxious, it's possible that the fourteen-year-old inside of you is rebelling against a left-over notion of bartered love.

MONOPHOBIA

The irrational fear of being alone (monophobia) may be the most devastating symptom suffered by women who are *Living Together, Feeling Alone*. These people are so removed from their own power centers that when they are alone they truly feel that there's *no one* home. Their fear forces them to endure ostracism, undue criticism, and other isolative behaviors coming from those whom they love. Because there's no rational basis for this fear, it's difficult to overcome.

The most provocative aspect of being alone is a person's reaction to silence. When you're cut off from external stimulation (sitting alone in a dark room), internal stimulation increases. When you're alone, you're more likely to become aware of your personality shortcomings, role conflicts, and painful memories. It's this awareness that astounds and often frightens. Furthermore, it can lead a person to ruminate on past failures, present disappointments, and future obstacles. It's then that abandonment becomes a threat.

Forty-year-old Sandy grew up in a rural part of Ohio, the eldest of seven children. Early in life, she became a "diaper changer," figuratively as well as literally.

When she wasn't caring for an infant, she was fixing dinner, cleaning up a mess, or breaking up childish spats. Sandy received little, if any, nurturance in return. Her only source of recognition came from her premature adult role.

"Dad was gone all the time," she said, "and Mom spent most of her time feeling sorry for herself. I took care of the kids more than my parents did. There was too little love in our house and too much competition for it. As the oldest, I was expected to give attention, not get it. I guess it sounds strange, what with all the kids and noise, but I can't remember *not* feeling lonely."

At fourteen, Sandy went away to a convent school to be a nun, more to belong than to pursue a religious vocation. "I couldn't stand the loneliness at home," she said.

After graduating from high school, Sandy left the convent and married the first man she dated, again motivated by wanting to belong, not by being in love. Her husband was good to her, but she eventually yearned to find something more in life. After twelve years of marriage and two kids, Sandy got a divorce.

Over the next ten years, Sandy lived with three different men, all of whom she thought she loved, none of whom made her feel that she belonged. Whenever she left one man, she did her best to find another one as soon as possible. By then, her fear of not belonging had become a fear of being alone. She organized her life so that she didn't have to confront the fears. Slowly, she developed monophobia.

The monophobe keeps herself so busy that she never has time to face being alone. She relishes demanding schedules, needy friends, and anything else that requires the consumption of time and energy. The only time she doesn't mind being alone is when she's too exhausted to care. "If I'm not talking on the phone," Sandy said, "or visiting with a neighbor, I keep the music blaring. The very thought of not having some noise around me drives me up the wall."

Although she may have a permanent relationship, a monophobe is more likely to have suffered several failed marriages or live-in arrangements. She rushes into her love life in order to avoid being alone and, consequently, makes poor choices about what kind of man to love (if she makes any choice at all). Monophobia can become so threatening that a woman will endure rejection in order to know that someone will be there when she comes home (sadly, the men in her life usually aren't there when she needs them the most).

Two weeks before our first session, Sandy had left thirty-five-year-old Brian, a man with whom she'd been living for four years. As in the past, she was plagued by the feeling that there had to be more to life than what she'd found.

Though she said that she and Brian were through, she was having considerable ambivalence about the breakup. She and Brian talked constantly on the phone about reconciliation. But it always came down to the same set of conflicts. She wanted a commitment; Brian just wanted to have fun. She felt that Brian didn't support her emotionally; Brian said that she was too needy. She was desperate for a man; he didn't want her clinging to him.

Sandy masked her phobia by saying that she was just trying to find a loving relationship. Her words were these: "I've always known that I was born to be a couple with a man." In truth, she didn't want to be coupled nearly as much as she wanted to avoid being alone.

Lessons for the Monophobe

- Silence can be provocative. In the absence of external stimulation, you become aware of internal stimulation, or "a voice from deep inside," as many people have called it. This "voice" can remind you of your faults, unresolved problems, and unsaid feelings. However, this voice can also lead you to your brain's power center. Be brave and listen.

- Monophobes often deny their fear by pointing to the time that they spend alone. However, during this time, they drown out silence by listening to music, calling friends, writing letters, and keeping busy with endless projects. You will not find your power center if you constantly create such noise.

- Don't judge yourself so harshly for being fearful. You may inadvertently take what often is creative energy and turn it into another attack against your self-esteem.

- Immaturity can cause a woman to believe that being alone will lead to uncoupled loneliness. The uncoupled, naive woman falsely believes that living with a man will automatically eliminate her low self-esteem and feelings of powerlessness. If she lives with a man without changing her focus, she'll just exchange one set of problems for another. Being with an insensitive partner can be much more painful than being alone.

SEXUAL INDISCRETION

Nowhere have the new expectations created more change than in the area of sexuality. Today's woman, feeling a new sense of sexual equality and pride, is taking more responsibility for her sexual feelings. Depending upon her sense of self-control and inner faith, she experiments with sexual fantasies, often finding new sources of pleasure as well as anxiety.

Excess and error are a natural part of the sexual awakening experiment. When the emptiness of loneliness is added to the confusion of role conflict, the resultant anxiety can drive a woman a bit further toward excess and a bit closer to error. I call that error sexual indiscretion.

Rita's is a case of a woman with low self-esteem who'd relinquished control over her own life and lost faith in herself.

Rita, thirty-six, wasn't the kind of woman who turned men's heads. Yet, she had a quiet attractiveness that could only improve with age. Her hair was short and lush, her green eyes twinkled, and her compact body suggested years of disciplined exercise. She avoided classic styles, preferring to dress in the latest fads. Her petite size allowed her to pull off the most outrageous of outfits. But her outward appearance did little to hide her inner pain.

Rita had worked as a massage therapist for almost thirteen years before going back to finish her college education. That's where she met Dick, her husband. They were married when Rita was thirty-three. Rita enjoyed her independence, but wanted to get married and have children. She got pregnant during their honeymoon, quit work, stayed home, and ''practiced being a housewife.''

After her daughter was delivered, Rita's idyllic life began to unravel. Dick worked three or four nights a week and Rita had neither the money for babysitters nor the desire to go out alone. She lost touch with her circle of friends and took up no hobbies. She was socially and emotionally isolated, and felt powerless to do anything about it. She became an LTL woman.

Rita, feeling more and more isolated and upset, told Dick that she wanted to return to work as a massage therapist. But, he said that he didn't want his wife having intimate contact with other men. Even though she assured him that she was a professional, they fought about it. Dick finally suggested that Rita set up a massage room in their finished basement, and work at home with a highly well-selected group of customers, mostly friends. Happy to have won a small victory, she gladly accepted.

Rita's first customers were their friends and neighbors. She felt better about herself, made a bit of extra spending money, and Dick didn't complain. Everything went smoothly for several months.

But then, Dick got a promotion and, in addition to being gone almost every weeknight, he started working weekends. Their social and sexual life practically disappeared. Rita still didn't have any friends of her own, and her attempts to confront Dick about her feelings and needs were met with him turning the attention to *his* needs.

''I didn't realize it at the time,'' Rita said, obviously deeply troubled, ''but I'd lost control over my life. I didn't have my own job, friends, or financial independence, and caring for my daughter just wasn't enough. I even had to work the way Dick wanted me to. Looking back, the loss of control explains how I let myself sink so low.''

''What do you mean?''

''Well, a new family moved into the neighborhood, and the man was immediately attracted to me and I to him. When he found out that I gave therapeutic massages, he asked me to help him with his bad back. I said I'd be glad to.

''During the first session, I could feel my heart racing whenever I touched his bare skin. When he turned over, I could see a bulge in the towel that covered him. The oils I use during a massage are very fragrant, you know, neither masculine nor feminine, just wonderful. I also keep the lights low and play meditation music. It's a very relaxing scene.

''Well, as I rubbed his feet, his erection grew and he gently asked me if I could help him with that problem. Before I knew it, I'd climbed on the table and we were having sex. He put some oil on my back and rubbed me slowly. I had the greatest orgasm I'd ever experienced. He, too, seemed very pleased.

''After a while, I got off of the table, put my clothes back on, and finished the massage. When he left, he kissed me warmly, thanked me, and gave me an extra fifty dollars. I know it sounds strange, but I didn't feel cheap. I felt terrific.''

Rita repeated this encounter two weeks later. Again, she'd felt very warm and tender, and had had terrific sex. She'd asked for no money, but was given a hundred dollars more than her usual fee.

''I remember looking at the money and saying,

'What's this?' The truth hit me hard. I was a kind, loving *prostitute*. It was difficult for me to admit this because I never thought of prostitutes as caring for the man nor enjoying sex the way I did. I hate myself for saying this but I miss it—not him, but the physical contact."

Rita's guilt over her sexual indiscretion was pushing her toward a nervous breakdown. True, she'd made an error in judgment, but it was understandable. Belonging is such a basic human need that, if it's not met, the resultant loneliness can drive a person to desperate acts. Rita had sought the most immediate and powerful antidote to loneliness—the human touch. She'd found momentary relief from loneliness in an act that was clearly outside her moral code.

Recognizing her powerlessness, regaining control over her life, and forgiving herself for a bad choice took a great burden of guilt off of Rita and made it easier for her to look to her future. She began to see that she'd turned to the man on her massage table because she'd felt disliked and unacceptable to the man with whom she was living, and cut off from all other avenues of belonging.

A Lesson About Sexual Indiscretion

• The human *touch* temporarily suspends loneliness; the human *encounter* triumphs over it. If you're having an affair or thinking of having one, reconsider what the real reason is behind your behavior. You don't want to get mired down in feelings such as jealousy, guilt, and believing that you love the man when, in fact, you're just trying to relieve your loneliness.

PHYSICAL AILMENTS

Ruth Lloyd, reporting in the health journal *Advances,* says that there are a number of studies presenting unequivocal evidence that "disease susceptibility and the genesis of health are, to a considerable extent, affected by the social milieu, the climate of everyday life." She further reports that a person's ability to adapt to life depends upon his or her "control over environmental challenge, or threat," and that the loss of control "can represent a significant stressor." Finally, she writes that stress "is likely to be associated with reduced immune competence."

In summarizing a wealth of research information, Mrs. Lloyd gives in-depth support to what James Lynch indicated when he wrote of *The Medical Consequences of Loneliness.* That is, if you have too much uncontrolled stress in your life, there's a good chance that you're going to get sick. Loneliness is an uncontrolled stress.

When she got married, Rita gave up her financial independence, including her own checking account. Her husband had wanted it that way. He'd told her that her job was to manage the house. If something broke, she was supposed to make sure that it got fixed. For the sake of love, she'd relinquished control over her own life.

Rita made a serious error in giving away her independence. She deactivated her power center and it faded into the darkness that was cast by her erroneous belief that loving someone meant giving up self-determination. It wasn't surprising to hear that she'd been having serious physical ailments recently.

"I've been having horrible bouts of vomiting, diarrhea, and fainting spells," she said. "I've gone to three doctors and each one told me that there's nothing wrong with me. And now, you're telling me that it could all be caused by nerves."

My response was guarded. "Living Together Loneliness is a chronic stressor, and unresolved stress is known to be correlated with health problems. I'm suggesting that your body *could* be reacting to the stress."

"Then it's possible, isn't it, that my physical problems are caused by loneliness?"

"Yes, it's possible."

Rita had been successful in the roles of co-worker and friend for over ten years, rarely experiencing the stress of loneliness, even though she lived alone. Now, just when she'd rounded out her life with a husband and child, she was forced to face a failed relationship, to encounter a seamy side of herself, and to subject herself to so much stress that her guts were literally coming apart.

A Lesson About Physical Ailments

• That loneliness is highly correlated with health problems is an established fact. That it can cause specific physical symptoms is probable, but not proven. It seems safe to say that overcoming loneliness is a highly desirable health-care goal.

OVERACHIEVEMENT/WORKAHOLISM

It's not uncommon for today's woman to hold down a job, pay bills, nurture a husband and children, participate in school, church, and community activities, see to the needs of her parents and in-laws, and carry on a vigorous exercise program. I know that to many of you, these activities seem normal and necessary. But I think they border on overachievement, and possibly even workaholism. When they do, they're a symptom of loneliness.

If a woman can do all this and still have sufficient time to maintain control over her life and nurture her need for spirituality, then fine, I'll relent and agree that she's a well-adjusted superwoman. However, there aren't too many of those kind of people around. To most of us, such a hectic schedule would push us toward burn-out, the end point of all stress.

Jill, the woman you met in Chapter 1, and again when I discussed narcissism, was an overachiever. In fact, it was her activities that I just listed. Jill sought me out because I wasn't a psychiatrist. She wasn't one to mince words. "You can't just give me pills, and tell me that I'll be okay. You *have* to talk to me. You have to help me find answers, not new drugs."

A major factor in Jill's loneliness was depersonalization. She performed many of her daily tasks as if she were working on automatic pilot, doing what she knew was right, but not feeling truly involved in it. She'd always been a "good girl," doing what was expected of her. It was the only thing she knew.

As a high school senior, Jill had been voted Most-Likely-to-Succeed. She'd been a cheerleader, class officer, and homecoming queen. Her teachers spoke of her great future, her neighbors told her how friendly she was, and boys fell over one another trying to get a date with her. She almost didn't notice that her parents, especially her father, were critical of her slightest mistake.

Listening to Jill detail how she overachieved in every area of her life convinced me that she was a workaholic. She *needed* her hectic schedule; it helped keep her mind off her loneliness. In fact, I've since learned that workaholism isn't restricted to the corporate man or woman who works eighty or ninety hours a week. *Housewives can also be workaholics.*

Jill was a success, at least according to the standards that had prevailed when she was growing up. She had a rich husband, two kids, a beautiful home in the "right" suburb, and a membership in a prestigious country club. She was a dutiful sister and daughter, a tireless community worker, and the one neighbor all others called upon when they needed help.

Jill had other things, too. Things that her classmates never thought of when they envisioned her success. She had an eating disorder, an alcohol problem, and an irresistible urge to sleep with the young tennis pro at the country club. Though overachievement was her dominant symptom, it wasn't her only one.

It would take Jill time to understand that her overachievement trapped her into believing that she could "get" belonging if she worked hard enough. She pushed herself to superhuman levels, all the while hoping that she could achieve her way out of loneliness. But it only got worse. Many women share Jill's faulty logic. That's why I believe that loneliness is the number one "disease" in America.

A Lesson About Overachievement

• Most overachievers push themselves beyond reasonable limits because they're trying to please someone else, not because survival demands it.

COMPULSIVE BEHAVIOR

If you have a quirky habit, such as not stepping on cracks in the sidewalk or knocking on wood for continued good fortune, it doesn't mean that you're compulsive. Compulsive people feel pressured to do the same thing over and over again, even when they try to resist it. Their compulsiveness severely disrupts their daily life.

The compulsivelike behavior that's a symptom of loneliness is usually much less severe than clinical compulsiveness. The two compulsions that I've observed in LTL women are the "Shop-till-you-drop syndrome," and what I'm calling "Cleanaholism." I found both of these in Jill, the overachiever.

Whenever Jill fell victim to one of Paul's isolating behaviors, she felt compelled to go shopping. Typically, the compulsion grew during the week and she acted it out on Saturday. She and her best friend usually spent about four hours shopping for clothes. She didn't come home until she had purchased several items, spending anywhere from one hundred to five hundred dollars.

Jill got a lot out of shopping. It released her pent-up frustration; she received enthusiastic peer approval for her endless variety of the latest styles; and it thrilled her to think of how upset Paul would be when he saw the bills (she always used credit cards). If, for any reason, she was unable to go shopping, she was upset. While she didn't become depressed or agitated, she did rearrange her schedule so that she could get a "fix" of shop-till-you-drop as soon as possible.

In many respects, Jill was an old-fashioned woman. She'd mastered the housewife's code: serve your husband and children's needs first; voice your opinions quietly; make your home his castle; and *never* make your husband look bad. What she thought was a credo for a happy life was, in fact, blind dedication to old rules that robbed her of independence. As much as she hated it, she was addicted to the servitude of the old rules.

Nowhere was this more apparent than in Jill's housecleaning habits. She was a "cleanaholic." While she didn't expect her home to be white-glove spotless, she did become upset if the main living areas of the house were dusty or slightly out of order. Because no one else could clean to her satisfaction, she never truly expected Paul or the children to help. Nevertheless, she regularly complained that they never helped her with the cleaning chores.

By embracing the traditional housewife role, Jill tried to find happiness *indirectly*. She hoped that a clean and orderly home would bring her recognition and belonging. While she found some enjoyment in having a clean house, she expected cleanliness to do more than it's designed to do—she wanted it to relieve her loneliness.

A Lesson About Compulsiveness

- A spotless world on the outside does little to keep
  your inner world orderly.

PART II

Treatment

WHILE there are endless shades of LTL feelings and many possible combinations of LTL symptoms, there are two traits common to all LTL women: they have an underactive power center and little faith in themselves. The result is an excessive reliance upon others, especially the man in their lives. Therefore, the treatment program for *Living Together, Feeling Alone* that grew out of Spiritual Behaviorism is called the *self-reliance program*.

There are five steps to overcoming loneliness through self-reliance: Surrender, Withdrawal, Reevaluation, Reemergence, and Discovery. They encompass a mixture of spiritual meditations and behavioral prescriptions. Surrender is a behavioral act, while withdrawal is a spiritual one. Reevaluation emphasizes inner growth while reemergence focuses on behavioral practice in the outer world. Discovery blends the spiritual and behavioral into a new way of life.

You could get the idea that each of these steps is a time-consuming exercise, separated from the others by weeks or months of work. There are no time frames on these steps. It took one woman a month to surrender herself to a situation. Another woman experimented with all five steps in less than an hour.

The particular time frame that you use will depend upon your history, your readiness to change, and your spirit of adventure.

Laura, the peacemaker, quit speaking her own mind because she believed that arguments would ruin her marriage. Rita, the massage therapist, in an attempt to find belonging, gave away her financial independence and, with it, her dignity. What they had in common was that in a rush to love, they forgot to take care of themselves. Maybe you have, too.

If you're *Living Together, Feeling Alone*, your loneliness acts as a driving force, moving you in one direction or another. You may think that by denying it, you'll stop the rippling effect. Not true. If you're an LTL woman, loneliness is an unavoidable part of your life *right now*. One obvious act, such as leaving him, will not reverse the process. You cannot control the fact that loneliness is moving you in some direction; you can, however, control the direction in which you move. Don't bother moving *away* from your partner just yet; work on moving *toward* yourself.

Your choice is essentially twofold. By admitting, even embracing, your loneliness, you can reactivate your brain's power center and renew your faith in yourself. By denying it, you'll "ripple" toward bitterness and emotional chaos.

Self-reliance does not mean that you'll no longer want or need other people, or that you're finally free from lonely feelings. However, future loneliness will be of the type that Dr. Zilboorg called lonesomeness (see page 20). Lonesomeness will not trap you because, when the pain comes, you'll know that it's the result of the choices you've made, not those that have been made for you.

6

Step One: Surrender

SURRENDER is the behavioral equivalent of prayer. Whatever the words or thoughts, prayer is an act of supplication to a power greater than yourself. Whether on bended knee or not, prayer helps you to reflect on yourself as a human being, and it brings you face-to-face with your inner self. When practiced as designed, prayer leads to greater strength, not weakness. So it is with surrender.

Surrender stops the chain reaction leading to loneliness before it gets started. Even though you may be emancipated and self-sufficient, some situations are bigger than you. When you surrender, you say, in effect, "I know that I can overcome nearly every obstacle, but I'm not invincible." You give up some of your old ways, or resist being part of activities that isolate you.

Your loneliness is an indication that your brain/soul connection is malfunctioning. The emptiness you feel is a passage, albeit a sometimes dark and frightening one, to a more productive, happier life. Don't deny your loneliness. Though it may be painful and frightening, it can't hurt you any more than it already has. In fact, it can help you, provided you surrender to it.

You surrender when you back away from your old ways, the ways that only frustrate you; when you admit that you're outnumbered by the factors that cause your loneliness; when you submit to your need to adjust your lifestyle. The only other alternative is to continue to ride into the valley of isolation where your self-esteem and belonging will be massacred.

I encourage you to begin your surrender to your humanity right now.

Raise both of your hands slightly, or envision yourself doing so, and then say out loud, "I can do many things, but I'm still a human being with human limitations." You've completed your first surrender.

SURRENDER WITH DIGNITY

Admitting that you're outnumbered is not the same as relinquishing your honor. *Your surrender is an act of humility, not of subservience.* You're surrendering to a situation, not another person. You recognize that you're not godlike, nor do you have superhuman powers. To surrender is to come to grips with the power of your spirit and the weakness of your flesh.

There's great dignity in this admission. In recognizing your limitations, you'll come face-to-face with your strengths. No, you can't stop him from turning a deaf ear to your concerns, or force your mother to be accepting and supportive; but you can refuse to subjugate yourself to such treatment. No, you can't always rid yourself of all the feelings of emptiness; but you can find increased belonging with yourself and with those who return your love.

There are many things that you can't do. And for each one you identify, you'll discover something that you can do. Use these four principles to surrender with dignity. (When you repeat these aloud as a method of self-support, they become mantras.)

- I have the power to change my life. But that power is not limitless.

- In order to harness this power, I must take action.

- I am free to choose different actions for different situations.

- I am separate from my man and not responsible for his life, and he's not responsible for mine.

SURRENDERING TO ISOLATING BEHAVIORS

Surrendering to your partner's isolating behaviors doesn't mean that you've abandoned your attempt to find belonging. It simply means that *in that situation*, in that moment, you've cut your losses, and moved away from it, to try again later.

Here are five mantras to use just before or during a surrender to isolating behavior. If you practice saying them now, they'll come to your mind more quickly when the isolating behavior is at hand.

- I can handle this, but not now.

- This is neither the time nor the place to confront this situation.

- There's more inside of me than I can show right now.

- The odds are against me right now.

- There's no such thing as winning an argument.

Each of these self-statements is like a prayer, reminding you of your limitations, yet encouraging you to keep a positive outlook on the future.

You can probably surrender to the overwhelming odds of a loved one's insensitivity before the day is over. The most important moment of this surrender occurs when you catch yourself thinking or acting in the same old, self-defeating way. For example, you jump to comply when he makes a demand, or you get defensive when he's critical.

When surrendering, you needn't raise your hands above your head, but I do urge you to incorporate a physical movement of some kind. I'd suggest making a time-out signal (forming a "T" with your hands), or holding your hands out in front of your chest, palms outward. You'll probably want to say something as you surrender. (Some women have found it best to signal surrender, but say nothing.)

Whatever you do with your hands, or whatever you say, be certain that, as you signal and/or talk, you take a small step *backward*, away from the situation, even if you're talking on the phone. This action reminds you to *disengage* from the situation. *This is the most important part of the surrender.* It reminds you that the situation is more powerful than you are *at that moment*.

Too often, when we encounter a frustrating situation, we take a step or two *toward* our antagonist. In doing so, we signal our combative intention both to him or her and to ourselves. It's nearly impossible to move toward an aggravating situation and not get caught up in it.

Your step backward needn't be pronounced. A small, barely noticeable retreat sends a kinesthetic (movement) message to your brain that says, "This situation is too big for me right now, leave it alone." It's difficult to maintain an argumentative posture when you're moving away from the situation. It also encourages the antagonist to cease his or her attack.

Your surrender will force you to accept some harsh realities. For example, you'll come face-to-face with the fact that love does *not* conquer all. Maybe it does when both parties' love is moving in the same direction, but not when one person won't work at it. Do not get caught up in a power struggle with insensitivity or ill-will. You'll always lose.

Earlier, I advised you to focus on what his isolating behavior triggered *inside* of you. Now, I offer you some things you might say while surrendering to the isolating behaviors listed in chapter 4.

- If you get the idea that you're a bother to your man, or you ask him to talk and he says, "What do you want me to say," surrender and say, "You win, I can't make you talk." It's not a surrender if you keep pushing him to talk or pressure him with Why questions.

- If your partner is demanding, raise your hands in front

of your shoulders, take a small step backward, and say, "I don't like being ordered around."

- If he belittles your friends, simply say, "It's too bad that you don't like my friends."

- If he's constantly critical of you, say, "I don't want to hear it." If he persists, you can continue your surrender by retreating to another room or, if necessary, leaving the house and taking a walk or a drive.

- If you're victimized by sexual manipulations, retreat from the situation and say, "I don't want anything to do with you right now."

- If your partner is emotionally vacant, if he won't talk about his feelings, back away from the conversation and say, "I need to talk about feelings. I hope you'll try to do that."

- If your partner is a blame-thrower, avoid becoming defensive. Surrender and say, "Don't throw the responsibility on me for this situation; it's not mine."

- If your man is a master at false contrition, you'll eventually find out that his "honesty" is just a manipulation. If you're suspicious of his contrition, surrender and say, "I'm sorry, but I simply don't believe you right now."

- If your love is rejected, say, "I can't continue to tolerate my love being rejected."

- If your teenager uses you as a scapegoat, if your sibling turns on you, or your parent seeks to manipulate you, refuse all arguments by saying, "I don't want to do this right now," "Let's stop this before it gets any worse," or simply, "You win."

When talking during a surrender, use sentences that begin with the word, "I." If you use "You" as the subject of your comment, you're in danger of being judgmental and that will only inflame the situation. If your surrender accomplishes nothing else, it will help you to avoid making a bad situation worse.

I can almost hear you say, "But he shouldn't get away with that," or "I shouldn't be a wimp when he's treating me that way," or "This isn't fair."

I agree that he shouldn't get away with it, but you can't stop him. Surrendering to your humanity is not being a wimp; if you argue, you'll never win. Of course, it isn't fair, but self-pity hurts you ten times as much as your partner's insensitivity.

If you believe that you can *make* your partner stop his insensitivity, and *make* him treat you with respect, you're flirting with narcissism ("I'm all powerful"), and will eventually end up feeling power*less*.

I realize that in the heat of the moment, some of my recommended comments may sound weak. But remember, while surrender is your prayer of humility, it's also a firm statement that you'll no longer tolerate isolation.

As you practice your surrender, you may hear yourself say, "This is stupid, it'll never work" or "How will this help my loneliness? I'm just giving in to his insensitivities." In fact, you are. You're surrendering to the fact that for the moment, the other person's insensitivity is stronger than your love.

When your fear of the future shakes your confidence, repeat this mantra:

• I will not permit this emptiness to continue.

When you're afraid of where your surrender will lead, be assured that it will lead you to a better place than where you are now. And, all of this can happen in *this* world. Be inspired by words sung by Reverend Purlie in the musical *Purlie*: "I want some glory *this* side of the grave."

Power Surge

If you pay attention to your inner feelings, the glory of self-reliance will begin seconds after a successful surrender. That's when you'll feel a real physical surge flash through your body. It originates in your brain's power center, but feels as if it's coming from your stomach. You feel a rush, a tingling sensation, as if a stream of warm water were running gently over your midsection.

The power surge results from a sudden awareness of inner strength. The act of backing away from a situation that overwhelms you builds your self-confidence, and you think, "I *do* have control over my life."

Your best chance to feel the power surge is when you refuse to argue. You raise your hands, take a small step backward, and say, "I don't want to do this." Then, you silently leave the room. The tingle will occur soon after your exit. You may even feel flushed as soothing oxygenated blood rushes into your newly relaxed abdominal muscles. It will only last a second or two, but the good feeling, psychologically, will last much longer.

Some of you may be unsettled by the power surge.

You may feel giddy or "rushed." Relax. You're simply experiencing something that you may not have felt in a long time—the power of self-control.

As you continue to generate the sensation of self-control by confronting bigger and bigger challenges you will be able to address long-standing, major unresolved issues. The more risks you're willing to take, the greater the odds that the tingle of building self-confidence will never end.

SURRENDERING TO YOUR SYMPTOMS

In addition to surrendering to isolating behavior, there are times when you must surrender to your symptoms. This occurs when a symptom becomes excessive, or so troublesome that it takes on a life of its own. When this happens, loneliness—the underlying cause of the symptom—takes a back seat.

Some symptoms of loneliness are more harmful than others. If you have a drinking problem, for example, it's not enough to say, "I do it because I'm lonely." This, indeed, may be true, but you must not let any shortcoming or symptom run your life. You must surrender to the symptom itself.

Alcoholics Anonymous asks its members to surrender when they say, "We admit that we are powerless over alcohol—that our lives have become unmanageable." If you have a drinking problem, I urge you to seek treatment (especially AA) and use your surrender to alcohol as a step toward healing your loneliness.

Another symptom that often calls for surrender is bitterness and blame. "All men are jerks," "Men are such babies," "Why do I always have to end up getting dumped on?" and "My isolation is all his fault," are just a few of the sounds of bitterness and blame.

As you'll recall, the principle of Hope tells us that all human responses start out as healing ones. The woman who uses bitterness and blame initially *intends* to use a harsh attitude to protect the tender feelings of the little girl inside of her (the feeling side of us is often referred to as the "child inside").

It doesn't take long, however, before bitterness and blame turn the little girl sour and she becomes nasty, even cruel. While I agree that feelings need to be gotten out in the open, sometimes—for example, when you're trapped in bitterness and blame—those feelings must simply be stopped.

If you have a lonely little girl inside of you and she's turning nasty, surrender to the symptom by taking a step backward from wherever you're standing (or lean back if you're sitting) and whisper "be quiet" or "hush." Do this whenever the bitterness or blame starts to well up inside of you. Don't permit yourself to be a blame-thrower.

This act of self-discipline will allow you to remove a self-protective device that you no longer need. You'll be better able to understand how your powerlessness caused you to slip into the habit of bitterness, and how bitterness and blame hurt you more than any person ever could.

You may also need to surrender to a sexual affair that's leading you nowhere. You can do this by stepping back from the man the next time you're with him (or retreating when you're talking on the phone), and telling yourself that your "addiction" to him is due to the fact that he touches you tenderly. Touch is an immediate antidote for LTL.

Thirty-eight-year-old Robin had known for years that her marriage was no good, but she'd stuck with it for the sake of her children. Her loneliness had reached a point at which she'd finally given in to a co-worker's sexual proposition. The sex was good, but the touching was great. When she found herself falling in love, she was riddled with anxiety. She knew that the man didn't love her, but she couldn't face giving him up.

Robin's first step in overcoming her anxiety was to surrender to it. "Imagine that you're trapped in quicksand," I said. "If you struggle by damning yourself for being there, you'll only sink deeper. If, however, you accept your condition as a temporary trap, you can relax and figure out your best escape."

"But," she said cautiously, "by surrendering, as you say, then I'm admitting that I can't do anything about the affair."

"No," I said, pleased to have a chance to clarify a common misconception, "it's just the opposite. You surrender to the overwhelming odds inherent in the fact that your loneliness is driving you into the arms of a man who only wants to have sex with you."

"So, by surrendering," she said, "I'm buying myself some time to figure the best way to pull myself out of the quicksand."

"Time," I said, "and an immediate increase in your self-esteem that comes from not damning yourself anymore."

Forty-three-year-old Doris, a wife, a mother, a saleswoman, and a monophobe, had the toughest of all surrenders. She had to surrender to the very thing that scared her—being alone. Until she quit running away from herself, she wouldn't have the strength to confront her husband's isolating behaviors.

Doris made a two-step surrender. First, while she was in the safety of my office, I instructed her to completely relax and breathe deeply and slowly. I then asked her to imagine being home alone and sitting in a similar chair. It took several trials before she could envision herself confronting the sounds of silence (no phone call, music, or other distractions).

Doris took the second step when she actually spent time doing what she'd imagined. She started out with one minute of quiet time and worked her way up to five minutes. This exercise triggered memories of childhood rejection and we talked about them.

It took several weeks of surrender before Doris could see how her monophobia created a chain reaction that resulted in her inability to confront her husband, Bill, for fear that he would leave her. As she gained some control over her phobia, Doris turned her attention away from her husband and to her childhood fears of rejection.

SIDE EFFECTS

Although surrender is a relatively simple act, it creates a chain reaction of its own. The power surge is just the beginning of what often proves to be an exciting ride on a roller coaster. There are, of course, downs as well as ups on this coaster. One of the downs is the possibility that you'll have a moment or two of mild panic.

Panic

"The last two days have been a nightmare," a visibly shaken Doris said. "The day before yesterday, I was driving to work and heard a news report that said a commuter plane had crashed. Bill was traveling in that part of the country, and I was absolutely convinced that he'd died on that plane.

"I pulled off to the side of the road and sat there in a panic. I cried, and kept saying over and over again, 'What will I do now? What will I do now?'

"I went back home, called a friend, and she helped me to find Bill. He was safe, but I was a wreck.

"That night, I had dreams of Bill dying in all sorts of accidents. I woke up feeling terribly guilty and called you."

"What are you guilty about?"

"You remember the first time we talked? I told you about sometimes wishing that Bill would disappear. I even had a fleeting fantasy that he'd die in a plane crash. Well, I'm certain that God is punishing me for that wish by promising to take Bill away from me."

"I'm no theologian, Doris," I said gently, "but I don't see God as a Being who takes love away when a person is in trouble. You may be confusing a Heavenly Father with your earth father."

"Then," she said nervously, "what's happening to me?"

"I don't know for sure, but my first idea is that the little girl inside of you is terribly frightened. You don't *wish* that Bill would die; just the opposite, you're *afraid that he might*. Then, you'd be left alone without anyone to protect you from your fear of being alone."

Soon after experiencing a surge of self-control, Doris

became complacent and quit working on her loneliness. She minimized the importance of the self-reliance program, seeing it as something she could do in her spare time. That had been a mistake. Her panic was telling her that she needed to make self-reliance a top priority. Only in that way could she find the security that she was so desperately seeking.

Fear

If you're a peacemaker, surrender will be especially difficult. You may erroneously believe that even a mild disagreement will lead to hateful, rejecting feelings. In that case, fear of disruption may cause you to sacrifice your integrity for the relationship.

If you have a fear of the confrontational aspects of surrender, evening may be the best time to try it out. During that time, insensitivity can prove especially provocative and surrender particularly helpful. Don't try to make your man talk, or turn off the TV. You'll never win. Say, "I wish you'd talk (or turn off the TV), but I can't make you." Then walk away.

Whatever you do, *don't* apologize if you hear an unfair criticism. When you apologize, you're saying, in effect, that your partner's criticism is legitimate, that you have a responsibility to answer him. For too long, women have believed that happiness was their responsibility, and that unhappiness was their fault. Don't let your fear drive you into that inescapable double bind.

Misuse

Some women misuse surrender by backing away when their partner confronts them with a reasonable concern or criticism. If this is you, examine yourself. Did you misread his comment and overreact? If so, honestly apologize and ask him to repeat his concern. Did you surrender as a tool of manipulation or as a way of expressing your anger? If so, tell him directly what you're upset about. If you don't clear up any misuse of surrender, your program of self-reliance will not work.

Depression

If you're an LTL woman, you have some degree of depression in your life. Surrender may stimulate more.

"My life is a mess, Dr. Kiley," Jill said, only slightly exaggerating her situation. "I drink too much, I'm having an affair with a man who I don't even like, and my marriage depresses me. I can't stand my life."

Jill, the overachieving, shop-till-you-drop woman you've met several times before, had to surrender to her humanity. She had to let go of years of living out the superhuman script, a script she'd inadvertently embraced when she converted her friends' and neighbors' compliments into a covenant. She'd viewed the title of Most Likely to Succeed more as a command than as a simple recognition of her talent and pleasant personality.

Jill's surrender washed away her denial and brought her face-to-face with her failures. The awareness didn't seriously harm her, but it did point out the necessity of rebuilding her life. Her sexual acting out, drinking, depression, and anxiety were all signs that she'd lost contact with her power center (as so often happens, there was some evidence that she'd never fully developed this invaluable resource).

Once you've completed your prayer of surrender, you'll have awakened your brain's power center and strengthened the integrity of your soul. Your next task is to retreat inside of yourself, experience the brain/soul connection, and nurture your spirituality with meditations on the principles of Truth, Hope, and Love.

7

Step Two: Withdrawal

DURING withdrawal, you retreat into yourself and embrace your aloneness. You replace your old lonely ways with solitary activities. You turn inward, get acquainted with your soul, and contemplate the three principles of Spiritual Behaviorism—Truth, Hope, and Love.

Don't be surprised if you feel yourself being pulled toward your dark side, toward confusion and uncertainty. Your faith in yourself will be tested, not because you have a terrible monster hidden inside of you, but because testing your faith is the only way to make it stronger. And it will get stronger. In fact, the only way that my recommendations won't help you is if you don't do them. If you feel your self-faith being shaken, don't worry, it's just the aftereffect of growth.

SOLITUDE, NOT RESPITE

When I tell LTL women to withdraw into themselves and spend time alone, many of them say, "I love being alone. It's no problem at all. I just don't get to do it very often."

A respite can easily be mistaken for solitude. But it's important to learn the difference between solitude and an hour or two of respite from a killer, stress-filled schedule. If you're up to your elbows in caring for kids, holding down a job, maintaining a household, helping with school or community functions, and worrying about your love relationship, the mere idea of finding the time for yourself may seem impossible. It's not.

While some stress is unavoidable and possibly even healthy, the LTL woman goes to an extreme. Her rush to satisfy everyone's needs results in her loneliness. When I suggest that she *regularly* spend time being alone, she rejects it, saying that she doesn't have time.

"*You* do my work," she'll say in mock sarcasm, "and then I'll spend time alone." Yet even when she has access to help, she'll find some excuse that'll permit her to do what she wanted to do in the first place—search feverishly *outside herself* for a relief from her loneliness. She never finds it because it's not "out there."

SOLITUDE

There are two dimensions to solitude: idling and solitary activity. While solitary activity is absolutely necessary for your treatment to be successful, time spent doing both is advisable.

Idling is a complete withdrawal from all worldly concerns. Looking at the clouds, walking slowly by yourself, or watching the rain are examples of idling. Your goal during idling is to minimize incoming stimulation, giving your brain a chance to rest. Idling can last from a few seconds to several minutes.

I've found two methods of idling that you might be able to use without taking any more time away from your busy schedule. If you ride the bus or train to work, grab yourself a window seat. Several times during your commute, find a point of continuity (a rail, the mid-stripe in the road, a curb) and stare at it as the vehicle is moving. Within seconds, you'll be caught up in a prehypnotic trance. Your brain is idling. Or, you can stare at the blades of a rotating ceiling fan. If your surroundings are fairly quiet, this will also result in idling.

Solitary activity is time you spend involved in a project that can be done by yourself. Solitary activities include needlepointing, cooking, reading, listening to music, or going out by yourself. Meditation is a special kind of solitary activity and it's very important in your progress toward self-reliance. Prayer might be considered a cross between idling and a solitary activity. Solitary activity can last as long as time allows.

According to research, aloneness is a source of adversity to many people. Because of the dramatic increase in internal stimulation, solitude can be frightening or agitating. That's because the central theme of internal stimulation involves those things we haven't yet resolved in our lives, our "unfinished business," so to speak.

A thought or a memory that causes you to have low self-esteem is a prime example of unfinished business. Solitude will bring those thoughts and memories into sharp focus. But since most people don't like to think about their problems, the byproduct of solitude can be upsetting.

I suggest that you use the *psych diary* technique to keep a running account of your solitude. Not only will it remind you to withdraw into yourself, but also it will help you to monitor the progression of thoughts and feelings during your withdrawal. Keep a notebook in a private place and write brief narrative descriptions of your thoughts and feelings at least once a day as soon after they occur as possible. A periodic review of your diary will guide your thoughts and suggest future actions.

Solitude is not a dangerous activity (with the possible exception of seriously depressed people who shun all social contact). Being alone won't create problems that you don't already have. It simply helps you to see your problems more clearly, facilitating resolution. Therefore, the adversity that solitude brings is also an opportunity for inner strengthening.

(An important distinction needs to be made here. If your depressive feelings are restricted to your relationship, then your primary problem is most likely loneliness, not depression, and you should proceed with my advice. However, if you suffer primarily from depression, my recommendation for solitary activities doesn't apply to you. Follow this general rule: If you're suffering from depression and loneliness, and if you have a *strong* drive either to be alone or to avoid being alone, you probably ought to seek professional advice.)

Solitude gives you the chance to confront the personality traits that cause your loneliness. If you study the material in this book carefully and permit yourself daily solitude, you'll eventually confront the cause of your feelings of emptiness and isolation.

Dedicate at least thirty minutes a day to solitude, with time allotted to both idling and solitary activity. Because it's often disturbing, you may wish to avoid solitude. You'll find it easy to "get busy and forget." If this happens, pull yourself back to the thirty-minute-a-day routine. Keep a checklist, if need be, to insure that you follow this recommendation.

BRAIN/SOUL CONNECTION

Most of us are able to grasp the concept of the brain's power center. I doubt if anyone knows exactly where it's located, but somewhere in our cortical gray matter is a safe bet. Most of us accept the concept of the soul, the driving force of our spiritual life. But to my knowledge, no human has ever seen a soul, nor does it seem to have a location. Most people think of the soul as being near our stomach; that's good enough for me.

George Bighorn, my American Indian mentor in "the traditional way," gave me a fascinating peek at my soul, which I've adapted into an exercise in Spiritual Behaviorism. Use the following exercise to "see" your soul, then follow me as I take you on a journey to examine the brain/soul connection.

During a moment of solitude, sit comfortably in a chair. Rest your elbows at your sides and put your hands out in front of you, slightly cupping your fingers. Now, put your hands together as if in prayer, but leave two or three inches of space between the palms of your hands. Let only the tips of your fingers touch one another.

With your elbows against your body and your hands remaining motionless, use your arms to rub the ends of your fingers together vigorously. Just a few centimeters back and forth is sufficient. Continue this for fifteen seconds.

Now, slowly move your fingers a few millimeters apart. Look at the space between your fingers and carefully notice the energy that seems to flow between the tips of your fingers. *That energy is your soul, the driving force beyond your mind and body.*

Rest your hands in your lap and shut your eyes. Use your imagination to follow your soul's energy down your arms and into your chest, lungs, and stomach. This is home to your soul. It's from your body's center that your soul provides you with your truth—*provided* you elect to trust your soul in deciding which choices to make.

With your eyes still closed, continue to use your imagination to acquaint yourself with the two parts of every person's soul—the male and female parts.

The male is located at or near your heart. When faced

with a choice, the male's job is to answer the question, "Is it (the choice) right?"

The female is located in the stomach area and her job is to answer the question, "How does this choice feel?"

Now, with your eyes still closed, continue your imaginary journey up your chest and into your neck. Picture yourself standing in the middle of your neck, about where the beginning of your windpipe is located. Look up and envision your brain, a marvelous computer more complicated than anything IBM has to offer.

See your brain as a receptacle of good and bad memories, genetic and cultural programming, early childhood conditioning, personality traits, and other bits of historical information. Realize that its job is to send information right past you and into all corners of your body.

Notice a tube running from a relatively small part of your brain directly to your soul. This is the connection between your brain's power center and your soul. As you already know, this center contains the problem-solving program that allows you to take control over your life. Your soul, especially the male part, regularly calls upon the power center for historical and moral data, and calculations that weigh opportunity with likelihood of outcome. The center offers the way, your soul provides the will.

As you stand there looking up at your brain and down at your soul, you can see how easy it would be for all sorts of extra information to trickle down to your stomach. The brain could easily flood your soul with excess data, especially if your power center is malfunctioning.

Now, travel back down into your stomach area and look around. Is your soul flooded with excess data? Is the male so deluged with gray conditional information that it's unable to give you a black-or-white, right-or-wrong answer? Is your female so burdened with memories of past failures and projections of future fears that it can't feel? If so, then you can't trust your soul to guide you in making choices. And, without trust in your soul, you can't have faith in yourself.

This exercise is difficult for some to master. If your imaginary powers are dormant it will take you a bit longer to see yourself in the positions that I describe. If you're a motion picture fan, recall scenes from the movies, *Fantastic Voyage* or *Innerspace*, and use them to heighten your travels inside of yourself. Or, do the same thing with clips from the television special, *The Brain*. The payoff of this exercise is worth the practice it takes to master it.

I encourage you to repeat this exercise as often as possible. Rub your fingers together and take note of the soul's energy. Follow that energy into your guts and greet your male and female parts. Ask your male if the proposed action is right or wrong. He will answer you. Then ask your female if the action feels right. She, too, will answer you. The more often you practice getting in touch with your male and female, the clearer their respective answers will become.

You'll be surprised at how the male and female parts of your soul cooperate. When something is right, but feels scary, or when something is wrong but feels exciting, your soul will tell you to do nothing for the moment. Only when both parts of your soul are in agreement, will you be motivated to act.

As you learn to trust your soul, your decisions will become easier. Your brain's power center will translate the new expectations into options, preferences, and logical guidelines. You'll trust yourself and you'll make the leap from the material to the spiritual, from knowledge to truth, without even realizing it.

MEDITATION GUIDE

Meditation is the purposeful direction of one's consciousness toward inner realities. It's like standing in front of a mirror and using your mind's eye to examine what you are and what you want to be. It's the consummate spiritual act.

Meditation is an essential part of withdrawal. Structure your meditation by reflecting upon the three principles of Spiritual Behaviorism. Create your own individual poster or sign (painted, needlepointed, stitched, typed) and hang it in a prominent place in your home. The sign should contain just three special words: *Truth, Hope,* and *Love*.

Find a quiet place where you won't be interrupted. You may decide to take a slow walk or simply sit in a chair (one woman had to "disappear" into her laundry room in order to find peace and quiet). Consider the explanations I'm about to give you. Contemplate how they might apply to your life. These meditations will nurture the seeds of self-faith needed to make the leap from the material to the spiritual.

Truth

The Truth principle is this: *All the answers to all your problems lie within you. Your task is to seek the information that will unlock those answers. Another person can only give you knowledge; you must find your own Truth.*

To consider Truth, listen to the words of my American Indian mentor.

"In the white man's culture, you believe that knowledge brings Truth. You are told that you must use your head to know and eventually you will feel the Truth in here." He points to his heart.

"Your pursuit of knowledge keeps you busy performing. To feel Truth, you impose your knowledge on others. When others don't accept your Truth, you are threatened and have no Truth in your heart. In order to feel whole, you must make others accept *your* knowledge as *their* Truth. You believe that others will not accept your heart unless they believe in your head. You are trapped, for you can never have peace in your heart.

"In traditional Indian medicine, we believe the opposite—the Truth in your heart must come first, then the knowledge in your head. We believe that you have always been a whole person. Since the day of your birth you have carried with you all the answers, all the Truth you'll ever need in your life. Your path should be to discover the questions that will unlock the answers that you hold inside. It's not knowledge in your brain that you must seek, but the Truth in your heart. When you are so busy seeking knowledge outside yourself, you have no time to seek the real Truth—that which is already inside of you.''

Take this philosophy and make a three-part mantra out of it. Repeat the mantra to yourself during your meditation, and find a way to incorporate it into your daily activities.

• Everything I see and hear is not Truth, only knowledge. Truth comes from inside of me.

• I must not force my Truth onto another person.

• I can only give people knowledge, not Truth.

Hope

The Hope principle is this: *Every human response to any given set of circumstances is initially a healing one. The healing response is always present though sometimes misdirected.*

To stimulate the growth of Hope, meditate on your inner goodness.

If you accept that Truth lies within you, and that the brain/soul connection is the mechanism for discovering that Truth, then the path to Hope lies before you. To get on the path, you must first accept your inner goodness, and then accept the fact that that goodness *always* tends toward healing and wellness.

If your inner goodness operates on erroneous information (for example, one of the old rules), you can get misdirected. When you sacrifice your integrity for love, you *think* that you're moving toward wellness. When you don't, you get confused and anxious and think that there's an evil force within you. You're wrong. In truth, you simply operated on false information.

(There are some in this world who either lack a conscience or intend to do evil [or both], but I'm not concerned about this small percentage of people right now.)

Hope will reside within you forever once you accept this corollary to the Hope principle: *If your decision is well conceived, your choice is automatically right.* Once you've looked at all the options, weighed the outcome with your morality, and listened to your soul, your inner goodness will take you in the right direction.

True, tomorrow you may change your mind, look at today's decision, and decide that it's no longer right for you. But that doesn't negate the correctness of today's choice. What you choose today is right for *today.* The reason that a day can make such a difference is that the strength gained in making today's decision gives you the confidence to consider options that may have been too frightening yesterday.

Once you accept your inner goodness, you'll always have Hope. Your brain/soul connection may get muddled and your healing response misdirected, but as long as you nurture your brain/soul connection and pursue Truth, your mistakes will always lead you to wellness.

Use this two-part mantra during your meditation:

- If I trust my soul and give myself the options, my inner goodness will always lead me to wellness.

- I don't make mistakes, I only learn to do things better.

Love

The Love principle is this: *The only reliable path to meaning in life is the construction and maintenance of intimacy between people.*

Love and intimacy can only enter your life through the door marked "Self-love." Meditating on the following imaginary journey will keep self-love in your heart.

Imagine yourself walking in the woods, your mind caressed by the intimate landscape. A gentle spring breeze tosses your hair as it washes away the winter's gray. You're alone and at peace. There's nowhere to go, so you're not in a hurry to get anywhere.

You wander aimlessly through a grove of gigantic trees, invigorated by the sight and scent of newly grown pine. You push back a curtain of green limbs and step unexpectedly into a clearing. Before you lies a magnificent meadow, tucked away from the world like a small child nestled in his bed.

The plush green carpet of grass is accented with richly colored flowers. You move toward a maple tree that sits majestically in the middle of the meadow. You sit down under the tree and nature tenderly cradles you. You'd like to doze but don't want to miss a moment of the wonderment.

Suddenly, from out of nowhere appears a butterfly unlike any you've ever seen. Its colors are vibrant. It dances gracefully in front of you, its wings whispering a spellbinding melody. You're touched by its significance. You know, without a doubt, that this is your butterfly. It's as if it came from a cocoon deep within your soul.

Instinctively you reach for it, but it frolics away. You stand and follow after it, for you know that it must not get away. It moves crisply and though you anticipate its path, your attempts to catch it prove fruitless. It's as if the butterfly wishes to be near you, but it knows that if you grab it, you'll kill it.

You pursue the butterfly to every corner of the meadow. When you reach for it, it pulls back; when you rest, it comes closer. Your confusion dominates as the day quickly passes.

You've spent all your energy and the entire day chasing the butterfly. Your exhaustion forces you to seek a respite. You retreat to the maple tree and "your" butterfly tirelessly follows you.

You lie back and close your eyes, seeking to find the peace that began that day. Within a moment, the butterfly comes to you and lands softly in the palm of your hand. You're too tired to move. You now possess it but it's still free. And then you understand. The butterfly is your self-love. If you chase it, you'll never have it. If you accept it freely, it will never leave you.

Practice this imagery just before walking into a roomful of new people when you're worried about acceptance, or entering into a evaluation session with your boss, or sitting in your therapist's waiting room, or just before confronting your partner about his insensitivity, or responding to your mother's criticisms.

This self-love mantra will help you to reach out to others.

- My self-love is always with me. I must not chase it away.

SPIRITUAL SUCCESSES

Lana, a forty-one-year-old regional saleswoman, worked the three-part mantra on Truth into nearly every business conversation. For example, she sat with a client who was going to buy a software system from either her or her competitor. Her closing statement went like this:

"I wish that I could convince you that our product is perfect for you. But I can't. *You* must make that decision. However, as I've already explained, this package incorporates the latest knowledge and technology that the field offers. If you decide that we have the right package, and then later need more help, be assured that I've got a lot of information at my fingertips to assist you. You can call anytime."

The client bought Linda's product.

Dee, a thirty-four-year-old, overachieving young woman, found a way to give herself eighty minutes of solitude every day without taking any extra time from an already hectic schedule. She followed my advice and sat next to the window on the side of the train that allowed her to gaze at the rails that paralleled the train during the fifty-mile-per-hour express run. After a few seconds of staring at one of the rails, she'd become aware of a flushed sensation in her stomach, similar to the power surge following a successful surrender.

This idling was especially important on her way home. By the time she walked in the door, she felt refreshed and better able to cope with her husband, Lyle's, insensitivity. She used the "hot tub" response to further cope with this problem.

As soon as she'd surrendered to Lyle's inevitably nasty comments, she told him that he'd have to handle things because she needed to relax. She then locked herself in the bathroom, drew a hot bath, put her favorite bath oil crystals in the tub, and soaked for about thirty minutes. I had suggested that she imagine herself on a tropical beach or sitting on a rug in front of a roaring fire. She also used this "hot tub" time to repeat the mantras of positive self-referencing. When she came out of the bathroom, she was much more capable of coping with Lyle's criticisms.

When Dee didn't take care of herself in this manner, she was victimized by her own bitterness. For example, should Lyle say, "Let me take you out to dinner," a tired and haggard Dee would sarcastically reply, "Wow! That's twice in ten years. Do you think you can afford it?" This, of course, would result in a blowup and a cancellation of the outing.

Although Lyle certainly wasn't Mr. Wonderful, Dee needed to realize that she had a history of connecting love to punishment. This made her *expect* abuse, even when Lyle tried to be nice. Sometimes, she even egged him on toward nastiness.

I suggested that Dee surrender to her bitterness, and institute a withdrawal specifically aimed at calming the nasty little girl inside of her. I appealed to her dramatic leanings by telling her to go to the cupboard after her surrender and get a candy sucker. She should then remove herself to a private area of her house, sit on the floor in a corner with a blanket around her, and slowly lick the sucker. She would, in essence, be nurturing the little-girl part of her, encouraging her to turn from being nasty to sweet.

The symbolism contained in this recommendation would help Dee with several tasks: to lend some structure to her withdrawal; to give positive attention to the child side of herself; and finally, to weaken the love-punishment connection by demonstrating that she didn't need to be nasty anymore in order to protect herself from rejection.

YOUR PERSONAL BOGEYMAN

Whether or not you had moments of fear during surrender, you'll likely have such moments during withdrawal. This fear is a direct result of turning your attention to your inner world. You might have flashbacks to moments from your childhood that still frighten you. You were afraid of rejection or abuse or being abandoned. You passed into adolescence and adult life without resolving these fears. In silence, they return. I suggest that they represent the quintessential nameless and faceless fear—the bogeyman.

If you have a personal bogeyman who sneaks up on you, and creates havoc with your peace of mind, use this exercise to protect yourself.

Sit in your favorite chair or lie in bed, and close your eyes. Take several deep breaths, hold them, and then relax the best you can. Picture yourself stepping into a time machine and being transported back in time, back to a time in your childhood. Back to a time that you remember as being difficult. See the situation and the people. Give it life—dimensions, color, and any face or faces you wish.

Now, focus on the things from that time that frightened you—the neighbor's dog, your Uncle Henry, your mother, your father, being left alone. Imagine that this fear is embodied in an evil creature, some diabolical denizen of the deep or a satanic monster. This is your personal bogeyman.

Remember that this is only an exercise and you can stop it any time you like. You are bringing the past alive and you can think about anything from your childhood that you wish. You control it.

Don't be afraid of your bogeyman, or to try to attack him. Just watch him. As you do, build a wall of clear light around you. Take your time. Let the light envelop you in a soft cocoon.

See the bogeyman dancing madly around the outside of your cocoon of light. He can't get to you. Tell the bogeyman that he can do whatever he wants, but he can't touch you. He'll try to sneak into your cocoon, but you needn't fear. He can't get in. Let him do whatever he wishes.

Think of every conceivable threat that your bogeyman could possibly conjure up, each time reinforcing the notion that you have the power within you to overcome your fear. Stay relaxed with that thought for a few minutes.

If you practice this exercise daily for at least two weeks, you'll be able to use it during the day when fear jumps out at you. Just let that wondrous cocoon of clear light envelop you, tell yourself that your bogeyman can't get you, then call upon your brain/soul connection to figure out your best course of action.

SIDE EFFECTS

Withdrawal sounds simple but it can be the toughest part of the self-reliance program. Here are two of the more predictable side effects.

Specific Fear

Your bogeyman represents a general fear that might hit you day or night. However, if you're monophobic, you obviously face a more specific fear—the fear of being alone. Since being alone is essential to the success of withdrawal, this step of self-reliance may be particularly difficult for you. If so, take your time. Remember, you must find your own Truth in your own way at your own time.

To overcome your fear of being alone, you may need a little help from the behavioral prescription of "desensitization." In essence, desensitization helps you to overcome your fears in small little steps. If you fear flying, for example, your first step is to look at pictures of airplanes, then go to an airport, then get on and immediately off an airplane, and finally take a short flight. Each of these steps is completed while you're relaxed, and you don't move on to the next step until you're comfortable with the previous one.

Doris, who had a fear of being alone, surrendered to her symptom, and was helped by desensitization. If you'll recall, she imagined herself confronting the sounds of silence while in the safety of my office. Once she could do this, she spent one minute alone, then two, and so on until she reached five.

She got totally comfortable with five minutes of quiet time, then worked her way to ten. Eventually, she was able to spend an hour or two in a solitary activity.

If you're monophobic, you'll need to create your own desensitization program to help you to withdraw successfully. Remember, move at your own speed.

Unneeded

Withdrawal may make you feel unneeded. And you might be right, at least in terms of you being needed to be someone's "whipping girl," or your partner's servant. If you increase solitary activity, some other activity will have to decrease. I'm hoping that this lost activity will be your needless tolerance of isolating behaviors.

If feeling unneeded is a problem for you, you'll find help in the role-review recommendation in the next chapter.

If you understand the fundamentals of tennis, golf, or racquetball, then you'll know what I mean when I say to envision surrender and withdrawal as your backswing. First, you move *away* from the ball in anticipation of your next shot (surrender). Then, at the end of your backswing, you hesitate for just a moment, reflecting on your shot (withdrawal).

Surrendering to isolating behavior and withdrawing into yourself prepares you for the next three steps of the self-reliance program: reevaluation, or properly moving yourself toward the ball; reemergence, or actual contact with the ball; and discovery, the awareness of what impact your swing has on the ball.

8

Step Three: Reevaluation

THE goal of the third step, reevaluation, is to strengthen your personality. This requires you to take a step back from yourself, examine your shortcomings, and make improvements where you see fit. Reevaluation is a spiritual act because you draw upon your self-faith in judging your behavior without judging yourself; it's a behavioral act because you must practice new action in the outside world.

The focus of reevaluation is to stop self-induced isolation; the focus of the next step, reemergence, is to stop others from isolating you. If you decide to follow one of my recommendations, do so by practicing the new behavior with a friend, neighbor, an understanding sibling, a stranger or a nonintimate acquaintance. Practicing new behaviors with an intimate, especially your partner, will increase your chances of rejection and isolation.

The end point of your reevaluation is to make a conscious commitment to change the rules by which you live. The way to begin your reevalution is to ask yourself two questions about the internal causes of LTL:

• Do I experience conflict between old rules and new expectations?

• Do I have low self-esteem, fear of anger, or feelings of narcissism and powerlessness?

If you're an LTL woman, your answer to both these questions is Yes. Let's take a look at them one at a time.

ROLE CONFLICT

Old rules are comfortable yet isolating; new expectations offer great promise but are scary. Unfortunately, you can't have it both ways. Either you opt for short-term comfort or long-term growth.

Below, I've again listed the old rules and new expectations. In chapter 5, I asked you to concentrate your attention on the old rules, and determine which ones you used to follow. Now, I ask you to turn your attention to the new expectations, and determine whether or not you can actively dedicate yourself to translating these expectations into new rules.

In each case, repeat the two statements aloud and ask yourself if they represent a conflict in your life. Then, reflect on my comments as you envision yourself behaving according to the new expectation. Do this daily, zeroing in on the ones that apply especially to you. Finally, ask the two parts of your soul which path you should follow. I expect that, in each case, your soul will choose the new expectation.

Old Rule One: Exercise control over a loved one, and you'll have belonging.

New Expectation: You are only responsible for yourself.

Think about the folly of controlling another. Each person has a free will, and no one has ever found a way to permanently circumvent this fact. Being responsible only for yourself takes an impossible burden off your shoulders.

Old Rule Two: Expect and tolerate insensitivity from a loved one.

New Expectation: Expect respect.

I know that you've heard this before, but you can't expect anyone to respect you until you respect yourself. If you respect yourself, you'll never again tolerate another's abuse.

Old Rule Three: One person should analyze a two-person problem.

New Expectation: Partners should solve problems together.

Despite what some television shows and some self-help books encourage, avoid playing the "junior shrink" role. You cannot solve a relationship problem by yourself, whether it be with your mother, father, sister, son, or partner.

Old Rule Four: Give unconditionally and you'll avoid rejection.

New Expectation: Sometimes, your needs come first.

If you've never done it before, it's a bit unsettling to place your needs first. When you make mistakes, others will quickly point them out. Despite the pitfalls of this expectation, the alternative leads to the very thing you fear—rejection.

Old Rule Five: Behaving perfectly is a way to find belonging.

New Expectation: You have the right to be wrong.

Think about it—if you expect yourself to behave perfectly, you're playing God. Furthermore, if you don't have the right to be wrong, you've excluded yourself from the human race. You're not God, but you won't let yourself be human. You end up being very lonely.

Old Rule Six: To avoid feeling lonely, avoid self-disclosure.

New Expectation: You deserve to be loved just the way you are.

Modern studies conclude that if you avoid self-disclosure, you isolate yourself. Not surprisingly, isolation leads to and exacerbates loneliness. There are people in your world who'd love to know more about the real you. Consider sharing more of you with them.

Old Rule Seven: Maintaining peace-at-any-price will turn away anger and create a sense of self-control.

New Expectation: You have a right to get angry.

Peace-at-any-price can turn you into a zombie. You mute your feelings, silence your power center, and crush your soul. If you subscribe to this way of life, you numb yourself in an attempt to find belonging. It won't work. You have a right to be angry; this includes getting unnecessarily upset. If this occurs, you can always apologize.

Old Rule Eight: When facing isolation and anxiety, acquire possessions, and the "right" friends.

New Expectation: Being alone is okay.

People who feel compelled to fill their life with acquaintances and things usually feel empty inside. More often than not, they're monophobic. The sounds of silence trigger the threat of the bogeyman, and they try to run away from him. Sooner or later, loneliness catches up with them.

Old Rule Nine: When the anxiety becomes too great, search for a simpler answer.

New Expectation: You have a right to be anxious and confused.

Anxiety is like a fever telling you that something is wrong in your life. Covering up your problems with oversimplified answers is similar to taking tranquilizers without working on the underlying problem. Giving yourself the right to be anxious and confused (or any other undesirable feeling) is a first step to finding out what's causing your stress.

Old Rule Ten: When all else fails, push the conflict and confusion out of your mind.

New Expectation: Your opinion counts.

With limited exception, denial is probably the most harmful of all defense mechanisms. The only time denial is good is *after* you've weighed the alternatives and made your opinion count.

If you choose to follow the new expectations, you'll need to improve upon your personality shortcomings before you confront isolating behavior.

OVERCOMING PERSONALITY SHORTCOMINGS

Following are ten positive actions you can take to overcome low self-esteem, narcissism, powerlessness, and fear of anger. These exercises will strengthen your personality and prepare you for reemergence, the most important step of the self-reliance program. Remember, you'll have greater success with these behavioral prescriptions if you practice them by yourself or with people with whom you're *not* emotionally involved.

Increasing Self-Esteem

Self-esteem can be a tricky subject because it's very difficult to define. Self-image, self-confidence, and self-assurance are all approximate synonyms for self-esteem. As you'll recall from chapter 5, your self-esteem is the sum total of your self-references; that is, what you say to yourself about yourself when you think of yourself.

It's not narcissistic to be concerned about what you think of yourself (narcissism is *exaggerated* self-concern). Realistic self-concern is vital if you're to achieve happiness and become a productive member of society. It's also indispensable if you're to overcome loneliness.

Examine the following list of negative self-references and see how often you say these statements to yourself.

I'm boring.

I wish I were a better person.

I'm not pretty enough.

I'm too fat.

I'm a bad wife (mother, daughter).

I'm a failure.

The more often you say these or similar statements to yourself, the more likely it is that your self-esteem will suffer.

The quickest way to increase your self-esteem is to increase your positive self-referencing. Talk to yourself in an approving way ("I'm an interesting person" or "I'm the best wife I can be"). Once you harness your potential and practice positive self-referencing, the strength will flow naturally.

Dedicate a part of each day to positive self-referencing. Use the mantras from your Surrender and Withdrawal to guide you. Research suggests that these things must be said out loud several times a day (any time will do—while brushing your teeth, combing your hair, driving to work, fixing dinner). You also might print or type them on a piece of paper and tape it to your mirror.

- I have the power to change my life.

- I am free to choose.

- I have the right to be wrong, to be angry and to have my own opinions.

- There's more inside of me than I can show right now.

- The only real Truth is within me.

- I don't make mistakes, I just learn to do things better.

- My self-love is always with me.

You can also find one or two negative self-references that dominate your thoughts and redirect them into positive mantras. "I'm boring" might become, "I have interesting things to say." Or, change "I'm a bitchy woman," into, "I can be a gentle person." Make sure that you repeat these positive self-references *out loud* ten or fifteen times a day. They needn't be shouted, just a whisper will do.

Accepting Compliments

Your self-esteem will also improve if you learn to accept compliments graciously. This means that your statements, "Oh, it was nothing" or "I really didn't do anything," should be replaced with "Thank you" or "I really appreciate the compliment."

Don't be unsettled by a compliment. You'll be tempted to think that you're being manipulated, but be selective in your evaluations. People with a high self-esteem can instinctively tell the difference between an honest compliment and a manipulation.

Although it may seem narcissistic, it's perfectly healthy *and* wise to give *yourself* compliments regularly. If you're a sports enthusiast, tell yourself, "Nice shot" or "Good anticipation" when performing well. Say, "tender roast" or "excellent sauce" when cooking, and "good work," "nice eyes," or "kind person" when going about your daily activities.

As you find ways of complimenting yourself, eliminate needless self-criticism. Too often, we yell at or belittle ourselves for a bad shot, thick thighs, or mushy vegetables. If you hear a voice telling you that it's not ladylike to pat yourself on the back, calmly tell that moralizing person from your past to be quiet.

Accepting compliments will reaffirm your right to intimacy, a right that loneliness can often make you forget.

Asserting Yourself

The most immediate effect of self-assertion is that it decreases your powerlessness. Over the long term, self-assertion will reduce your narcissism and fear of anger.

Practice the following self-assertions with a nonintimate friend.

- Apologize for a mistake without continually explaining why you did what you did. A simple, "I'm sorry for what happened" is sufficient. This is a very powerful antidote to the narcissism.

- Say No to an excessive demand, without offering a profuse apology or explanation.

- State your opposition to another's action or to an institutional policy or law simply and clearly.

- Make a request that someone help you with something or with meeting one of your needs.

- State your anger rationally and calmly. "I'm really disgusted you did that" or "That behavior turns me off completely."

Self-assertion reduces the chances that your anger will turn to rage. Rage backfires on you because your man will point to your hysteria in dismissing your concerns, or simply ignore you because he couldn't hear your needs over the noise. Asserting your thoughts and feelings before you're ready to explode increases your chances of being heard.

Increasing Self-Disclosure

The research literature seems clear in showing that the absence of self-disclosure (talking about your inner feelings) leads to loneliness. But what is not clear is when, where, and with whom you're supposed to disclose your feelings. The challenge of self-disclosure is in answering the question, Whom do I trust with what kind of information, under what circumstances, and how far do I trust them?

The only successful way to answer this question is through a modified version of desensitization. That is, you move very slowly in disclosing sensitive information to people in whom you hope to trust. Follow these rules when increasing your self-disclosure.

- Ask your soul if the person in question is trustworthy. Your soul may not give you a clear answer, but you'll get a hint. Follow it.

- Use remote feelings first. That is, talk about your feelings from a year or two ago rather than yesterday. Then, talk about yesterday's feelings before sharing today's.

- A few hours after the sharing, ask yourself how you feel about disclosing the information. If you feel good, share more feelings; if not, back away.

- Pay close attention to the other person's reaction. If he or she listens and is supportive, that's a good sign. If he or she is critical or judgmental, that's a bad sign. The reaction of others is crucial in determining whether self-disclosure is helpful or harmful.

- Self-disclosure opens you to rejection. If you feel rejected, back away. Later, ask yourself if the rejection you felt was due to the other person's criticism or to your overreaction. If the other person is supportive and kind, and never uses your shared infor-

mation to belittle you, then he or she is likely
trustworthy.

- Don't apologize if a friend says, ''Why didn't you tell
me this earlier?'' Your answer should be, ''I didn't
feel good about sharing this before.'' You don't owe
more of an explanation than this.

- If a trusted person ever uses your shared information
against you, or belies your trust, realize that you made
a mistake trusting that person and learn from it.

Self-disclosure increases your risk of rejection, but it
also gives others the opportunity to know and love the
real you.

Reaffirming Financial Independence

I've repeatedly found that the LTL woman fails to attain
or maintain her financial independence once she becomes ''attached.'' If your financial independence is in
question, you needn't immediately rush out and get a
job or improve your income. But, you must ask yourself
this question: Could you, if you had to, go out into the
world *tomorrow* and survive financially?

If the answer is No, then you have some work to do.
Update your résumé and call a couple of employers;
maybe you'll realize that you're in better shape than you
thought. Take a couple of classes at the local college,
or ask for a promotion. Get a credit card in your name,
take a class in financial planning, and make sure that
you understand last year's tax return. Reaffirming your
financial independence may be nothing more than
opening your own checking or savings account.

Whatever the course of action you take, make sure that you're not ignoring the fact that, in the final analysis, you must take care of yourself in this world.

Shaping Up Your Health

While you're shaping up your financial life, do the same thing for your body. Loneliness is very stressful, and it's easy for LTL women to put their physical health on the backburner. As you've already learned, this can be a deadly mistake.

Make a commitment *today* to improve your health. With the consultation of your physician, take some stress vitamins and implement a sensible diet. Then, get out of your chair and exercise. Ride a bike, take a brisk walk, swim, or attend an aerobics class.

(Being that I'm an avid handball player, allow me to convince you to take up the sport. Exercise physiologists consider it to be the most comprehensive exercise. You get a full-body workout, you develop speed, power, endurance, and mental discipline, and you get to enjoy competition. You wear gloves, the ball is softer than it used to be, and hearing and feeling the "smack" of hitting the ball does wonders for your stress. Women in handball? You bet!)

The payoff of a reasonable health-care program is endless. You feel better about yourself, have more energy, and more optimism about taking control of your life. Needless to say, as you improve the quality of your life, you may also be improving the quantity of it.

Expanding Internal Control

The LTL woman tends to see herself as victimized by forces beyond her control. She is "externally controlled," believing that chance has a greater impact on her life than does choice. The classic example of an attitude of external control is the person who doesn't bother with defensive driving because he or she believes that accidents are caused by fate.

Expand your internal control by practicing the "I-am-something-without-a-man" exercise. Once a day, talk about your life to a friend for ten minutes without making any reference to a man. Focus on your hopes, dreams, spiritual beliefs, or philosophy of life. This will help you to see *yourself* as the most important influence on your future.

Here is a mantra about choice that may help:

• No matter what path my life has taken, I've always had a choice in everything that I've done.

Those who'd argue that this is an extreme statement, that a choice between two evils is not really a choice, have a point. However, even when your free will is severely limited by the threat of death, you still choose—you choose life.

The main reason I support this mantra is that in taking responsibility for *all* the decisions in your life, you give yourself greater access to your brain's power center. You're able to forgive others their transgressions, to let go of the need for blame, revenge, and self-pity, and to look to the future with great anticipation.

If you follow the choice mantra, you'll find the power to sort through the causes of your loneliness and choose to maximize your self-reliance. Remember: *Your loneliness begins with how you love, not how he acts.*

Practicing Opinions

Your internal control will be enhanced and your powerlessness decreased if you practice stating your opinion about the things you encounter during the day. What's your favorite car, color, or building? Do you like chicken better than steak; red wine better than champagne? Do you favor long hair or short hair, big dogs or little ones?

Practice giving your opinion as often as you can throughout the day. You can tell it to a friend or co-worker or simply say it to yourself. It works best if you say it aloud. Giving your opinion exercises the brain/soul connection, preparing it to confront much larger issues.

SIDE EFFECTS

If you're going to suffer any negative side effects during the self-reliance program, they're most likely to occur during reevaluation. When you confront the conflicts in your life, or seek to make changes in your personality, you shake the foundation of your daily behavior. If your balance is precarious, there's bound to be some fallout. Let the experiences of other women support you.

Disorientation

If you decide to give up your old rules in favor of the new expectations, you can expect some period of disorientation. Listen as Jill, the affluent overachiever you've met several times before, described her lost feeling.

"I've lost my entire self," she said tearfully. "I don't enjoy being a wife at all, my kids act like ungrateful little shits, and I'm even bitchy to my best friend. Other than my work, I don't have anything that gives me pleasure. I don't even know who I am anymore."

Jill was describing the emptiness that had resulted from reevaluating the superhuman script and deciding to let go of it. She didn't want to be a superhuman anymore, and once she decided to change, she started throwing away most of her old roles and beliefs. In a sense, she had to construct a new personality, a most difficult task.

"I don't see how I can construct a new life and stay married. Paul complains about me 'changing the rules,' and I haven't even gotten a good start."

"What about your fear of not having money, and of being alone?"

"Those things still scare me, but nothing can be worse than the way I'm living right now."

Throughout much of her conversation, I noticed that Jill was starting most of her sentences with the words, "I feel . . ." or "I know . . ." This indicated to me that her sense of alienation was dissipating, and that her feeling of isolation would soon follow. (If you'll recall, persons suffering from alienation tend to speak in a passive voice; that is, "The steak was good," instead of "I liked the steak.")

"You're making progress," I said, after explaining how a more active voice would lead to a more active power center.

"Oh, wonderful, Dr. Kiley," she replied with a twinkle in her eye, "I'll tell myself that the next time I feel like dropping out of life and going to a convent."

If you suffer from disorientation, take heart. The healing process will not abandon you. Once Jill let go of her superhuman script, she was left with the natural strength that came from seeing her inner goodness and realizing that there was power in simple survival. It will be the same for you.

Anger

If you overcome your powerlessness and fear of anger, there's a good chance that you'll become aware of angry feelings that you've never expressed. Forty-six-year-old Rosie had some trying moments when she became strong enough to face her unresolved anger toward her mother.

"My mother wasn't competent to have five children," the petite redhead said, her eyes spitting fire. "She got in over her head and used me, as the oldest, to bail her out. I had such anger in me this past weekend that I nearly exploded. Finally, I was so upset that I visited the cemetery and spit on her grave. It sounds terrible, but I feel better."

Rosie's mother had kept her so busy caring for her four brothers and sisters that Rosie never got to be a child. Consequently, she had never worked through the trials and tribulations of adolescence and therefore wasn't prepared for adulthood. Her pent-up anger was understandable.

Rosie's surrender and withdrawal gave her the strength to reevaluate her life. She permitted her anger to surface, and it was expressed by her symbolic act in the cemetery. We used that action as a jumping-off point to talk about her childhood frustrations. Resolving past anger made it possible for Rosie to put her present anger in better focus. She was able to quit blaming her husband for her loneliness and to confront him about his isolating behaviors.

Painful Reminiscence

If you successfully complete the first three steps of the self-reliance program, you'll be willing to investigate other areas of your life. This will likely lead you to reminisce about your childhood. Because you have increased strength to face the truth, not all of that reminiscence will be happy.

Forty-four-year-old Eve had been reared in an atmosphere of bartered love. Her father had played the part of a loving Daddy, but in truth, had been a cold man who demanded that things go his way.

About two weeks after successfully surrendering and withdrawing from her symptoms, Eve began to reminisce about her childhood, and how the attitude of bartered love had been programmed into her life. Her trip down memory lane brought back a lot of painful recollections.

Eve recalled that her mother always deferred to her husband on matters as simple as what she must buy at the store. Eve remembered being petrified of her father's disapproval. Although he always bought her everything she wanted, he would remind her regularly that he only loved her because she appreciated the nice things he gave her.

"I realize now that there was a string attached to his love," Eve said, crying softly. "He expected absolute compliance with his wishes on every score. Otherwise, he would take his love away.

"One time shortly after I was married, I thought I was pregnant. I knew that Daddy would not want me to have a baby so soon. By the time I found out that I wasn't pregnant, I'd made all the arrangements to get an abortion."

The more Eve surrendered to the forces that overwhelmed her, and withdrew into the sounds of silence, the more she understood the devastating effect of bartered love. Eventually, she realized that one reason she hadn't recognized her loneliness was that it had become a way of life; she knew nothing else.

You've reached a critical point in your treatment. You must decide if you're ready to change the rules by which you live. Ask your soul that question right now, and listen carefully for the two-part answer. If the answer is Yes, proceed with the next step. If the answer is No, or if there's considerable hesitancy, *that's fine*. Put the book down for a few days, and then ask yourself the question again.

Your soul is telling you that you're not ready to move on. *That's your Truth*. Follow it. You have unfinished business to take care of. Maybe you haven't surrendered as completely as you should, or spent enough time in solitude, or been thorough enough in your reevaluation.

This treatment program will help you overcome your loneliness. But *you* must decide the pace at which the program proceeds. If you've validated your soul, it will not let you move ahead until you're ready. Don't let *my* knowledge substitute for *your* Truth.

9

Step Four: Reemergence

You've surrendered to overwhelming odds, withdrawn into yourself, and reevaluated the whys and wherefores of your life. These three steps will prepare you for the real work: reemergence. During reemergence, you'll "come out of your shell," so to speak. You'll test out new ways of behaving.

The goal of reemergence is to resolve the conflict between the old rules and new expectations by establishing new rules. The new rules will allow your brain/soul connection to flourish. Reemergence occurs as you return to situations that isolate you, looking for other, more effective ways of reacting.

Trial-and-error learning will be your constant companion during reemergence. Certain words will feel better than others; certain actions will prove more effective than others. You should feel free to experiment with words and actions, applying your new expectations to old problems.

As you experiment with new ways of relating to your man, remind yourself once again that *you* are the primary cause of your loneliness. You're only using certain situations that happen to involve him, as a practice field to better prepare yourself for life, with or without him. If your relationship improves as a result, all the better. If not, you'll have to worry about that later. First things first—and your loneliness comes first.

ROLE REVIEW

Anytime you take on a difficult task, you should warm up. The best warm-up for reemergence is a role review; that is, reviewing the roles you play in various life situations. Role review permits you to take a look at your overall lifestyle. The following outline of a role review gives you the necessary guidance.

First, list all the roles you have in your daily life. Here are the major ones:

Mother	Worker
Daughter	Grandmother
Wife	Friend
Lover	Volunteer
Sister	Neighbor

Next, think of the person(s) with whom you have the most contact when you're in that role. Your partner, children, parents, boss, sister, and best friend come immediately to mind. Ask yourself what you want or need from these people.

Then, spend a few days reviewing recent situations

involving those roles and ask yourself some questions. Which roles are successful and which are failures? Try and pinpoint the words or action that led to the outcome, regardless of whether or not you like it. What did the other person say or do that made you feel good? Bad? What comments or actions stimulated feelings of rejection, isolation, or estrangement?

The more intimate the relationship, the greater the chance for satisfaction or disappointment. True, you may have an irrational fear of rejection from your neighbor or a coworker, but the fear will have a greater impact on you in a relationship with someone you love.

Finally, examine your behavior in different roles and use your more successful roles to help bolster your more ineffective ones.

Using role review as warm-up is like sitting in the grandstands watching a game before you begin playing. You examine the players' strategies, footwork, mistakes, and successes. You try to identify what it takes to achieve victory and avoid defeat. Warming up to the game is obviously not the same as playing it, but it's certainly better than simply being thrown into the fray.

Role review was instrumental in the development of thirty-five-year-old Nancy's self-esteem, and eventually, her new rules. The raven-haired accountant studied the list of roles, and decided that being a friend gave her the most satisfaction. We reviewed her friendship behavior and found that two things made her a good friend: She listened well and she lovingly confronted her friends when she thought that they needed it.

Nancy completed the role review process by identifying other roles in which she could listen better and improve her confrontation. She immediately improved her mother role by listening more to her kids and confronting their disruption more directly.

SEVEN NEW RULES

Following is a review of seven rules that will help you avoid the LTL experience. I call these rules "new" because they flow from the new expectations discussed earlier. The rules are not foolproof nor should you adopt them without first subjecting each one to careful scrutiny. The process may help you to discover other rules, ones more applicable to your unique needs. It will take time to develop new rules that work for you. So, once again, don't rush yourself.

New Rule One: Stay in your Adult when confronting isolating behavior.

Transactional Analysis (TA) is an approach to human behavior that instructs us to view our behavior as a product of the interaction among the Parent, Adult, and Child parts of our personality. The Parent is our conscience, the Child embodies our feelings, and the Adult is our rational self. The TA counselor will suggest that the Adult, by giving and receiving information, monitors the activity of the Parent and Child so that they stay in balance.

Twenty-eight-year-old Stephanie, a vivacious and up-and-coming advertising executive, often played the Parent to her husband, Mat. When Mat was self-pitying or when he belittled Stephanie, he was operating from his Child; when Stephanie lectured or demanded, she was responding from her Parent. Their Parent-Child communication was destroying their relationship.

I told Stephanie to respond from her Adult when Mat was being a Child. This required her to either request or give information. So, when Mat said, "I wanted to go out tonight, but I guess we can't because you're mad at me," Stephanie should avoid telling him to grow up and, instead, *request* information by asking, "What do you need from me?" If he persists in his Child, she should *give* information by saying, "I don't want to talk about this right now." If he still remains in his Child, she should terminate the conversation.

Isolating behavior will come from your loved one's Child (self-pity, temper tantrums, unfounded anger) or from his or her Parent (excessive criticism, judgmental attitude). You'll be tempted to respond from either *your* Child or Parent. This new rule tells you to stick with your Adult. That is, either request or give information. If, in the course of this activity, you learn that the other person is unwilling to respond in a rational manner, your Adult should end the conversation.

Special note: The peace-at-any-price attitude comes from your overzealous Parent. The biggest damage it does is to force you to tolerate unwarranted criticisms. These criticisms are like so many nails driven into the coffin of your power center. Call upon your Adult in changing your peacemaker role.

New Rule Two: Be specific in requesting what you want.

The old rules touted passivity as a positive feminine trait. Women were to be pretty, be patient, be home, and be quiet. You didn't need to worry about requesting anything because men, in their infinite wisdom, always knew exactly what you needed, nothing more, nothing less.

It takes assertiveness, internal control, self-esteem, and humility to admit that you have needs and to request that they be met. Asking for what you want demands that you expect respect, put your needs first sometimes, and make your opinions count.

New Rule Three: Give yourself quiet time.

Even if you become the most self-reliant person imaginable, you'll still need time to yourself. Any person who cares about you must understand this. So, not only must you give yourself permission to spend time alone, you must also inform your loved ones of your needs. Help them understand that your quiet time does not mean that you care about them any less. Maybe you can even help them learn the benefits of solitude.

For example, tell your five-year-old, who's banging on your bedroom door, that you're having adult time; and your husband, who interrupts your hot bath with financial problems, that he'll have to wait.

New Rule Four: Take responsibility only for what is yours.

Envision responsibility as a hot potato. If you don't know how to hold it, it can burn you. It's tempting to try and toss it to another person. If you're willing to take responsibility for what's not yours, you can bet that there are plenty of people who'll toss the hot potato into your lap.

A stressed partner will blame you for his bad day if

you allow him to. Your teenager will say that he lost his girlfriend because you grounded him. Your father will blame you for his loneliness if you try to assume the role of his social director. If you send out signals that you'll handle other people's responsibility, you'd better be ready to juggle a lot of hot potatoes.

When you take responsibility only for what is yours, you refuse to catch another person's potato. Imagine yourself standing up when your partner throws his hot potato toward you. Instead of grabbing it, cooling it down, and returning it to him (he probably won't take it back), see yourself as dodging the potato and saying, "Hey, you dropped your potato." Your actual words might be, "That's not my problem, but I'll help you if you wish."

"I'm pulling back from trying to control the important people in my life," an excited Ginger explained, "and I've never been stronger." The thirty-two-year-old, sandy-haired woman had sought help because she dealt with powerlessness by trying to control people.

"I thought that letting go of control would result in rejection," she said, "but just the opposite is happening. I've made more friends recently than at any point in my life."

I pushed Ginger to specify the changes she'd made in an effort to help her pinpoint the reason for her success (so that she could continue it). Together, we identified several significant changes in her attitude and behavior.

First, Ginger reminded herself not to be so quick to ask people personal questions (for example, she previously would ask a brand new acquaintance why she'd gotten divorced). Her questioning was viewed as intrusive. People became offended because they didn't understand that Ginger was worried about disapproval and had inadvertently fallen into the trap of seeking instant intimacy.

Ginger also improved her health care by reducing the fats, sugar, and caffeine in her diet, and increasing her aerobic dancing. Gaining more control over her physical condition gave her more security and improved her self-esteem.

Most important, Ginger quit taking responsibility for everyone's problems. She quit apologizing to her husband when it wasn't necessary, and quit explaining her actions to her mother when it was clear that Mom just wanted to complain.

"I can't tell you how important that Cherokee Indian's philosophy is to me," she said sincerely. "I've always tried to force my Truth onto someone else. If they didn't take it, I felt rejected and tried even harder. Now, I can relax and offer my knowledge, knowing that I have no power over what another person does with it."

New Rule Five: Never argue.

This may sound strange, but you can eliminate arguments from your life immediately. That's because arguments are one of the few interpersonal situations that you can control. It takes two to argue, and if you refuse to be a party to an argument, there won't be one.

The strategy needed to implement this rule is as follows. Surrender to the initial outburst without leaving the area; find something in the other's comments that you can agree with; state that agreement without passing judgment; finally, remain silent, with or without leaving the area.

Here are two scenarios in which this strategy might apply.

Your husband blows into the house after work and says, "Why didn't you clean up the yard like I told you to?" You back away from this accusatory comment, raise your hands slightly, and say, "I don't want to argue."

He counters with, "You never want to talk when *I* want to." Stifle your desire to say, "But you only want to argue," and say instead, "You're right, I don't usually want to talk when you want to."

Now comes the most critical part—*remain silent*. You needn't leave the room. But be aware that your actions are stressful to your partner. He's charged up for an argument and you're not playing the game. However, you're not doing anything that destroys the possibility of a sincere conversation either.

The ball's in his court. If he pushes the argument, you may repeat your strategy or simply walk away. If he drops it, wait a few minutes and then ask him if he wants to talk now. If the two of you talk, great; if not, leave the area.

Follow the same procedure when your fifteen-year-old daughter tries to bait you into an argument. It begins as soon as you say No, or she anticipates a No to her request.

"No," you say firmly, "you may not go to that party Saturday night."

"But, Mom," she wails, "*everybody* will be there."

Resist the temptation to challenge this teenage terror tactic, and reply, "I guess that might be true." Then, *remain silent*. Turn your attention away to a simple task, like washing your hands or getting a drink of water.

New Rule Five works hand in hand with New Rule Four. If you use the anti-arguing strategy to cope with loved ones who bait you, you'll have a much better chance of avoiding the hot potato of responsibility.

New Rule Six: Resist a lying touch.

Nothing can induce loneliness like a touch that's supposedly given in love and concern, but actually is a lie. Being the recipient of a genuine hug immediately suspends any loneliness that you might have. However, if you find out later that the hug was, in truth, only an attempt to manipulate you, your loneliness deepens as does your suspicion about future hugs.

Fifty-year-old Alice had always been very insecure. Over the years, she'd permitted her husband, David, to treat her as a second-class citizen. She never had the courage to confront him until she discovered that he was having an affair. She described what happened the second night after the blowup.

"I tried to talk to him about our future, but he wouldn't talk. I was sleeping in the guest room, and he woke me up about 3 A.M., said he wanted me, not her. We had sex, and he went to sleep. When I wanted to talk the next morning, he said that I should forget about it, because he had. He thought that having sex made everything okay."

David was using intimate physical touching as a way of manipulating Alice. He wouldn't talk about their problems, but then expected her to think that having sex made everything better. Alice, in permitting David to use a loving touch in order to perpetuate a lie, naturally felt doubly cheated and abused. Her mistake had been in agreeing to sex when there was a major rift between the two of them.

If you feel that your man only touches you when he wants sex, use my "ten-second kiss rule." Suggest to your man that once or twice a day, you engage in a passionate kiss for ten seconds *without* any genital contact. This rule helps a man become sensitive to the benefits of an embrace without sex.

New Rule Seven: Let some problems simply fade away.

Just as there are some problems you should talk about, there are others you should permit to fade away. You should talk about a difference in religion, you should let a disagreement over pork chops versus chicken fade away. Discuss bad feelings generated during a trip to his mother's house, but forget about whether or not your Uncle Harold is a penny-pincher. Child-rearing issues should be worked through, while rare and ill-timed comments about your hair can be disregarded.

Thirty-one-year-old Susan, a housewife and mother, was driving herself toward a nervous breakdown by insisting that she and her husband, Chuck, had to resolve every little problem that came up. When Chuck made a disparaging comment about her new dress, Susan couldn't let go of it, even after Chuck apologized.

Susan still remembers the argument that she and Chuck had over the correct name of a new neighbor. Chuck had had a difficult time admitting that he'd been wrong, and Susan gloated over it for days. She continued to bring it up whenever they disagreed over something.

Susan's reevaluation and reemergence taught her that she could protect herself from isolation. As a result, she learned to let small problems fade away. Her only difficulty was learning to discriminate between small and large problems. She relied upon her soul and trial-and-error learning in overcoming that hurdle.

Clearly, time does not cure all relationship troubles. But in some cases, it's the best medicine. The challenge, of course, is knowing when to resolve an issue and when to let it go. One course of action is to leave a conflict alone for a few hours and see how you feel. If it fades away, great; if not, then there's a reason why it won't leave. Find out what it is.

SIDE EFFECTS

The side effects of reemergence are not nearly as troublesome as those that come with reevaluation. However, you can reduce what side effects there are by remembering to forgive yourself for the errors that come with trial-and-error learning.

Worry About Failure

Most of you have heard of Murphy's Law: If something can go wrong, it will. My adaptation of that law is this: Never again worry about whether or not something will go wrong, because it will.

Moreover, the best time to learn is when you've made a mistake. If you do something correctly, there's no learning involved because you already knew how to behave without error. But when you make a mistake, you're usually motivated to find out why, and when you discover your error and correct it, you've learned something.

Once you've made your best choice, and taken the most decisive action you possibly can, cast your fate to the wind. If the outcome is positive, that's fine; if not, you've learned something. Your power center picks up valuable information for future use. And, you've given your soul a lesson it will not forget.

Forty-year-old Sue's reemergence officially began when she was discharged from the substance abuse program. She was petrified of what other people would say, of returning to alcohol and drug abuse, and of once again suffering from low self-esteem. Each one of these things represented a threat to her adjustment.

"You really don't have to worry about whether or not you're going to have bad days," I said, attempting to lighten her burden. "Things *will* go wrong, and you'll have bad days."

Sue had to accept this inevitability. But she had plenty of resources to call upon if she did get into trouble, and people who genuinely cared and would help her any way they could. She was able to accept this help only when she realized that her surrender to alcohol and drugs was never-ending.

The End of a Relationship

If your self-reliance is successful, there's a chance that your relationship will not survive. Remind yourself that you chose to take care of yourself first, and let the relationship fall where it may.

Forty-seven-year-old Barbara, a divorced physician, focused her reemergence on a constructive confrontation of her relationship with her live-in partner, Thomas, also a physician. Barbara had worked hard to gain control of the frightened little girl inside of her. She'd also had to contend with a strong history of practicing Old Rule Two, expecting and tolerating insensitivity. The confidence she'd gained during her treatment helped her face the possibility that her relationship, something she dearly wanted, might not survive.

She planned social outings with Thomas, his friends, and their wives. She took a greater interest in his research job, asking him to brief her on the scope of his problems. She surrendered and withdrew from his criticisms, and introduced the subject of their faltering sex life when she sensed that he was in a good mood. She even tried to get interested in professional football.

Barbara's actions made her feel better and they contributed to a more peaceful household. However, Thomas didn't respond as Barbara had hoped. He remained critical and self-involved.

"What are you going to do?" I asked.

"Trust my soul," she answered calmly. "If the relationship ends, I know that it's for the best."

Friends' Reactions

When you stop being everything for everyone, your friends and loved ones will wonder what's wrong with you. They've come to expect that you'll serve them without complaint. The ones who truly care will understand when you tell them that you're changing the rules, and that you're learning to take as well as give. You should have patience with those who are willing to adapt, and don't waste time on those who won't.

When Jill, the superwoman you've heard about several times in the course of this book, reemerged from a difficult reevaluation, she was faced with a delicate social scene. She was ostracized because she broke with the expectation that women who marry money shouldn't expect to have love too. In opting for love, Jill threatened a lot of social customs in her circle of "friends" and many of them publicly criticized her. The husbands of those same "friends" called and offered their support, but were unable to mask their sexual intentions. She spent a lot of nights alone, listening to music, reading, and crying. She was very lonesome, but had begun to escape her LTL.

You've surrendered to isolating behaviors and symptoms that overwhelm you, withdrawn by meditating on personalized mantras, reevaluated your personality, and reemerged with new rules of behavior. Your loneliness should have abated.

Check your progress by retaking the survey of feelings (page 44). If your score in any one of the five categories exceeds 20, reread the appropriate explanation in chapter 3, "The Stages of LTL," and reevaluate your symptoms (chapter 6). (If only one score is over

20, but shows a significant decrease, continue with your program and retake the survey in a couple of weeks.)

Then, complete another role review, looking for situations that trigger the feelings you've rated the highest. Finally, refocus your treatment on those situations. If you feel the need for additional support and guidance, call a friend, your physician or minister, and get a referral to a competent psychotherapist.

Do your best to explain the LTL treatment program during your first session. If the therapist has a method of reevaluation and reemergence that's different from mine, that's okay, provided you're comfortable with it. However, if he or she will not support the surrender and withdrawal part of the treatment, *do not go back*. These two steps must be carried out as designed.

Five or six supportive therapy sessions is all you'll need to stay on the track of self-reliance. If, however, the therapist, without coercing you, is able to show you that you have a more complicated problem, or if you feel as if you're profiting from therapy and don't want to stop, then, by all means, continue.

(The best way to choose a therapist who's right for you is to determine whether or not he or she follows the three principles of Spiritual Behaviorism, especially the one governing Truth. If a therapist tries to make his or her knowledge your Truth, run for your life.)

10

Step Five: Discovery

THE goal of step five is to permit the work you've done in steps one through four to take you on a journey of self-realization. During your journey you'll continue to discover new attitudes about yourself and life. You'll gain deeper insights into yourself and your partner's behavior. You'll have a greater freedom to explore new activities and attitudes because you're no longer ashamed of the "error" part of trial-and-error learning. Discovery occurs naturally and never really ends; it just melds into self-reliance.

This chapter is dedicated to sharing the discoveries made by several of the women you've met in this book.

YOUR SOUL'S NOT ALWAYS SURE

Stephanie, the advertising executive, who needed to stay in her Adult whenever she confronted her husband, Mat, discovered that her soul wasn't sure about what she should do when it came to her marriage.

Once Stephanie was no longer running away from herself, she faced some big decisions. Should she and Mat remain married? If so, what could she do to improve the relationship? If not, what should she do and how soon should she do it? Should she switch jobs? Which job should she take?

I helped Stephanie through each of these decisions, constantly reminding her to trust her soul.

"But my soul isn't certain," she said, under pressure to make a decision about moving out on Mat. "My soul is saying, 'Don't do it,' but then I think my soul might be wrong."

"Don't expect your soul to give you absolute certitude," I replied. "Just look for a direction."

"But I can't get a clear message."

"Then don't do anything. If you face a situation in which something must be done, give it your best shot. If your trial results in error, trust your soul to recover. Try not to be in such a hurry."

One last thought meant a lot to Stephanie during her treatment. It was: Your soul will take you where you need to be; however, where you *need* to be is not always where you *want* to be.

FAMILY SUPPORT

Alison, the housewife and part-time bookkeeper, identified herself as an adult child of an alcoholic, but resisted treatment. Her husband, Hunter, recognized that his life had become indirectly dependent upon alcohol, but he, too, was reluctant to face his codependency.

Alison's withdrawal led her to the realization that she

needed more time outside of the home. She spent too much time worrying about her two children and her relationship, and too little being involved in life. As a result, she expanded her eight-hour-a-week job to full-time. Hunter and their children agreed to take more responsibility for running the household.

She also increased her self-esteem by confronting the household ghosts. She took a giant step forward when she gave herself permission to grab a frozen dinner and tell the refrigerator to shut up (she actually said, "Shut up!").

Alison's greatest triumph, however, came when she bought a small shelf-size ironing board and threw away the big one her aunt had given her. She swears that she heard Aunt Tody's ironing board screaming as the jaws of the garbage truck crushed it into oblivion.

Alison's progress on her substance abuse was painfully slow, two steps forward, one back. After a year and several relapses, she admitted that she was abusing tranquilizers as well as alcohol. Shortly thereafter, she voluntarily entered a thirty-day, inpatient substance abuse program. Hunter and the kids attended family counseling sessions. During our last conversation, she said that she was free from tranquilizers, but had had two bad drinking days in the past three months.

When sobriety did come, it enabled Alison to take a more objective look at her life. She realized that, in search of recognition and acceptance, she'd overdone the mothering role. Supervising her two children was necessary, but she'd taken it to an extreme with her son, Scot. Her low self-esteem had indirectly accounted for her overparenting.

Conversely, Alison had avoided the roles of friend

and neighbor because the increased possibility of rejection made her nervous. Also, she realized that she drank in order to find the courage to open up to what few friends she had.

The good news is that Alison is a regular attender of Alcoholics Anonymous, and she, Hunter, and the two kids are attending regular family counseling. They air their gripes, share their concerns, and do their best to support each other. Together, they've discovered a sense of bonding, of being able to talk about anything and work it through. More than once Hunter and the kids have expressed their unwavering dedication to helping Alison, without becoming codependent as they were before.

"What's your biggest discovery thus far?" I asked Alison.

"That I have a family who cares for me."

"That, dear lady, is the stuff that power is made of."

GOING TO OPPOSITE EXTREMES

Not all the things that you'll discover during your post-treatment period will come up roses. This is especially true of the first six months. As you go through the transition from the old rules to the new ones, you may find yourself going to extremes in searching for a new balance.

Thirty-seven-year-old Linda, the dazzling, energetic woman who was a major proponent of Old Rule Seven—maintain peace no matter what the price—discovered the extremes of love relationships.

"I've never been in a healthy relationship," the

bright-eyed blonde said. "I'm not sure what I'm doing. Sometimes, I feel as if my expectations about people and life are off, as if *I'm* the one who's still wrong."

After enduring years of loneliness, Linda had divorced Jimmy, and now was involved with a man whom she dearly loved. However, she was concerned about her lack of tolerance for some of his behavior.

"The other day, he was acting silly and I wanted him to be serious. He made one too many jokes and I yelled at him, and told him that I didn't need his immaturity, and then I stomped away."

Linda's man may have been a bit too silly, but in her push to be self-reliant, she'd overreacted. In the past, she'd been a spineless peacemaker. Now, as she experimented with the new expectation, "expect respect," it was understandable that she might go to the opposite extreme.

Linda had spent countless years wallowing in low self-esteem and powerlessness; once she accepted the challenge of growth, she was very sensitive to any kind of immaturity, either in herself or in those she loved. Her overreaction unsettled her, making her think she'd gone from being a peacemaker to a bitch.

However, her "bitchiness" was only a momentary side effect of her adjustment to a new way of living. Because she accepted trial-and-error learning, she eventually saw her error and apologized, this time appropriately. It took Linda several months before she found a comfortable balance between assertiveness and empathy.

One of Linda's new rules was, "If I become uncomfortable, I'll tell my man immediately." What she had failed to add, and what she was now learning, was this corollary: Sometimes, the problem may be me, not him.

A BAG OF ROCKS

Vivian was the woman you met in the section on fear of anger. She'd been treated as a non-person by both her father and her husband, Jack. In fact, Jack was cruel to the point of abuse.

Vivian's trek toward self-reliance eventually led her to an attorney's office where she sought a separation. She didn't actually sign any papers, but the mere act of having them drawn up was a clear signal that her fear of her own anger was coming to an end.

When she told Jack about seeing an attorney, he was stunned. He said that he didn't understand why she'd done that, a statement Vivian couldn't believe that he'd said with a straight face. She also was relieved to realize that her fear about Jack's explosive reaction was groundless.

Unlike many women who might have seen fifteen years of marriage as a "waste," Vivian had a very insightful viewpoint about the years she'd spent trapped in LTL.

"I don't feel as if my married life was a waste," she said. "Everything was important at the time I did it. It had to be the way it was. I had to go through all those painful stages. I wanted to leave several times, but I didn't understand why. I now know that if I had left, I'd have felt guilty and forced myself to return. Who knows, maybe then I would've been trapped forever."

I'd told Vivian about the respect that the American

Indian has for nature. I'd shared with her my special attachment to mountains. Our conversation led to one of Vivian's most astute discoveries.

"You know," she said with a warm smile, "Jack was a bag of rocks that I was trying to carry over my own personal mountain. The bag weighed ten times what my strength could lift, but I was determined to get that bag over that mountain."

"You were determined to make him into a caring, loving person," I said.

"Exactly. I now know that that will never happen, at least with me as his wife." She grinned broadly and I thought that she looked ten years younger than when I first met her.

She continued. "I finally dropped the bag, knowing that I'd never succeed. I feel kind of bad about it, but my shoulders don't hurt anymore. I'm very excited to go on by myself."

Vivian completed one survey of feelings the first day I saw her and another the day after she finally signed her separation papers. Following is a comparison of those two scores:

	First Day	After Signing
Bewildered	30	12
Isolated	23	4
Agitated	27	8
Depressed	27	5
Exhausted	29	4

Vivian is a classic example of how quickly an LTL woman can turn her life around. In a matter of a few months, she'd moved from being a helpless victim of Jack's insensitivity and of soul-piercing loneliness to a self-reliant, fully functioning person, complete with signed separation papers and renewed hope.

"How did you do all this so quickly?" I asked.

"I guess that I gave myself permission to get angry and to take control of my life. The rest just seemed to happen."

Vivian surprised me during our last conversation. I'd expected to hear that she was proceeding with a divorce. Instead, she informed me that, although she knew her marriage was over, she'd decided to take the summer off, live at home, and have Jack support her.

"I'm sitting in the sun, reading, playing with my kids, and sleeping in the guest room. Jack is busting his rear to please me. I'm not sure how long I'll do this, but it feels good right now."

AGREEING TO DISAGREE

Fifty-year-old Alice had endured a life with no parents, her own immaturity, her husband David's demands, and his lying touch. I was surprised that they'd stayed together. However, at this point, things have improved and Alice isn't ready to get a divorce.

Alice's level of agitation, depression, and exhaustion dropped dramatically, a fact she attributes to a major change in her self-control. "I now feel more in control of my life," she said. "Before I faced my loneliness, I had little or no self-control. And that put my self-esteem at a very low point.''

Alice's Bewilderment score was still relatively high, a fact she explained this way: ''There isn't a clear relationship between David and me, but we still live together. That's very confusing. I'm a 9 on 'uncertain' because I have no idea what's going to happen to us. He's finally agreed to go for marriage counseling, so maybe we can still have a marriage.

''My feeling of emptiness has dropped considerably while my feeling of being excluded has jumped up to 10. That's because my self-esteem has improved to the point where I have the courage to see the truth—I really *am* excluded from his life.''

Before she began treatment, Alice felt that she had no right to be in disagreement with David. If he was upset or bothered by something she'd said, she felt guilty and was compelled to explain herself until the two of them no longer disagreed.

Once she realized that he had some significant shortcomings and that she could disagree with him without feeling like a bad person, she was able to say to David, ''Well, on this topic, honey, we're simply going to have to agree to disagree.''

If Alice continues to strengthen her power center, and David improves his communication skills, there's no telling what their marriage might become. No one has ever challenged David before, so even *he* doesn't know what changes he might make.

AN INNER TOUGHNESS

Rita was the thirty-six-year-old massage therapist whose loneliness had driven her into sexual indiscretion on the massage table.

Rita's anger score dropped from 40 the first time I saw her (that's the highest possible score), to 12 the last time. She pointed to two reasons for the change: no more self-blame for the massage-table sex, and a feeling that she was doing something about her marriage.

That something was asking Dick to leave. He'd been quite reluctant at first, and had not complied until she consulted with an attorney. Before leaving, he'd made some very derogatory, even threatening, statements to Rita, vowing to seek revenge on her for kicking him out.

Rita's tough reaction had surprised even her. "I told him that I wouldn't take that crap from some spoiled little hypochondriac. Then, I went to the sheriff and had a peace bond put on him before his trail was cold. Two days later, he's all sweetness and light, saying that he loved me so much that moving out drove him nuts. I told him that he was nuts a long time before I kicked him out."

Rita divorced Dick two months later, and six weeks after that, began to work as a massage therapist again. She's now returned to her independent lifestyle, dates men who are kind and attentive both in bed and out, and is studying to be a physical therapist.

THE FUTURE IS UNCERTAIN

Sandy, the monophobe who'd been a diaper changer throughout her adolescence, discovered that she could live with an uncertain future.

"I've moved back in with Brian, but I still don't know whether or not we'll make it. I sincerely hope we do. But he has to start doing some of the work. I've quit being his mother, nursemaid, confessor, and whipping girl, so I'm excited to find out what he'll do now."

The final chapter has not yet been written on Sandy's relationship with Brian. Just when I think that they're heading for a strong commitment, they return to their old ways, and everything blows up. But, Sandy recovers quickly. She's learned that self-reliance isn't an *endpoint*, it's a *process*. So, when she feels herself losing control, she surrenders, withdraws, reevaluates, and reemerges, better able to trust that her soul will lead her to discover the truth that she needs.

I'd love to be able to tell you that Sandy and Brian will make it. But my crystal ball is on the blink.

"I'm sure that some of my friends think I'm stuck up," Sandy said during a recent conversation.

"Why's that?"

"I don't call them as often as I used to, or get together with them."

"Why not?"

"They interrupt my silence, and without my silence, I don't know who I am or where I'm going."

So much for Sandy's monophobia!

BE READY FOR ANYTHING

Laura, the woman whose isolation had resulted in alienation, enjoyed considerable success in the self-reliance
program. She was particularly pleased that she'd learned
how to confront her husband, Kevin's, unwarranted
criticisms.

Three months after taking a hiatus from counseling,
Laura returned, complaining that she was once again
reacting to Kevin's criticisms. However, things were a
bit more complicated this time. She was still living with
Kevin, but had begun to have an affair with Rod, a co-
worker. She returned to treatment because she was confused about her feelings.

After several sessions, she decided to surrender to
her confusion and withdraw from both men. In order to
give herself plenty of solitude, she moved into her own
apartment. We both agreed that she should not see either man. She needed to get to know herself, but was
unable to do that while living with a man.

Though both Kevin, her husband, and Rod, her
lover, called her regularly, Laura remained firm in
her pledge not to see either of them. The fact that she
had little trouble avoiding Kevin, but wanted desperately to be with Rod, forced her to reevaluate the
future of her marriage. She filed for divorce and re-
sumed seeing Rod, spending most of her evenings at
his apartment.

Much to her chagrin, Laura returned to counseling
several months later. Although she hadn't officially
moved in, she was now spending every night at Rod's
house, and was once again experiencing LTL. She said
that she'd gone to the opposite extreme with Rod, dom-

inating him much as Kevin had done to her. She was still battling the attitude of "I'm not a likable person."

Laura discovered that she had to stick with the self-reliance program no matter what kind of progress she supposedly made. Given her ongoing struggle with the peace-at-any-price philosophy, she also decided that at the moment, she wasn't ready to live with any man. Furthermore, she thought it ill-advised to even date. So, she resolved to return to her living-alone, celibate lifestyle.

That decision lasted exactly ten days.

"I met a man yesterday," she said matter-of-factly. "He's married, he said he'll never leave his wife, and I'm going to have an affair with him. I'll have a source of sexual maintenance and won't have to worry about getting a disease or screwing up another relationship. It's a little risky, but it's my comfort zone."

Psychotherapists learn early in their careers to be very careful in making predictions about a person's behavior. However, I was 99 percent certain that Laura's marriage to Kevin was finished. I was wrong. Two months later, Laura made still another turn in her search for a productive relationship.

"Is it still a surrender," Laura asked me during a telephone follow-up, "if Kevin belittles me, and I don't respond at all?"

"Not only is it a surrender," I said enthusiastically, "but it's the ideal goal—to make no response to destructive comments. Why do you ask?"

"Well, I've been seeing Kevin, and whenever he tries to hook me with one of his zingers, I totally ignore him and turn away. He's treating me decently and I'm going to move back in."

I smiled to myself, once again humbled by the fact that human behavior never ceases to amaze me. I then asked Laura to brief me on this surprising development.

Laura had ended her sexual-maintenance affair, made a pact with Kevin that they would both stop drinking, and then implemented her no-response approach to his nasty comments. As a result, she and Kevin talked more than ever before, and, though their sex life was still practically nonexistent, they did hug and touch each other warmly.

"I notice a big difference in both myself and Kevin when I ignore his childish responses. He seems to shape up immediately, and then we either talk about what happened, or go on about our business. I'm thinking that maybe our relationship just might work out."

I strongly suggested that Kevin and Laura make a commitment to ongoing marriage counseling. When Laura said that Kevin thought that they could make it on their own, I became adamant in my dissension.

"You two are up against overwhelming odds. There is a history of horrible communication, emotional abuse, and the absence of intimacy, not to mention your propensity for peace-at-any-price. If you don't get regular counseling, your relationship will continue to be one that's managed by crisis. Please don't let that happen."

Laura seemed firm in her resolve to make a counseling appointment and do everything short of coercing Kevin into going.

"I admire you for trying to make your marriage work. If Kevin works as hard as you are, you two just might make it. But remember, you can always change your mind. Just trust your soul."

JILL'S NEW IDENTITY

Jill, the thirty-nine-year-old woman you've followed throughout this book, needed to construct a new identity, one free from the narcissistic superhuman script. Although we talked at length about the importance of trial-and-error learning, she still found it extremely difficult to accept flaws in her personality. Her history of trying to be perfect was very strong and unforgiving.

Once Jill had accepted her perfectionism, it began to change, and her new identity emerged rapidly. She moved out, filed for divorce, and changed jobs. Because she lived nearby, she was able to work out a plan with her husband for joint supervision of their teenagers.

Four months later, a revitalized Jill had a new circle of friends, an even better job, an improved relationship with her daughter, and a twenty-eight-year-old boyfriend.

"At first, I was apologetic about dating a man who's twelve years younger than I," she said energetically. "But, he's caring and attentive, and certainly a better lover than my ex-husband ever thought of being. Anyhow, we're just having fun and I love it."

Jill gradually became aware of a new set of rules that would govern her relationship with men in the future. Among them were:

• I refuse to be with any man who isn't nice to me. That includes good manners.

• I expect warmth and intimacy from a partner. If I

don't get it, I'll talk about it. If I still don't get it, he'll be out of my life.

- We will talk about our problems, each admit our respective mistakes, each agree to change, and then go on with living.

- I sometimes want to be held without him expecting sex.

- I want my time alone to be respected.

- I want him to think of my needs and feelings.

"I was driving to work the other morning," Jill said, obviously delighted with the story she was about to tell me, "and I come up behind this guy who was jogging alongside the road. I was going slow so I had plenty of time to check him out. 'Nice buns' I said as I came alongside him. 'Cute' I said as I passed him. Then, I did a double-take. It was Paul! My ex! Then, I got mad. He'd lost forty pounds, had his teeth fixed, changed his hairstyle, and was wearing designer running shorts. I thought, 'I asked him to do all those things, and he ignored me.' "

"Were you tempted to go back to him?" I asked.

"Are you kidding, Dr. Kiley?" Jill said, looking sexy enough to attract any man she wanted. "Just because a package has a pretty ribbon doesn't mean that the present is any good."

At first, the five steps to self-reliance should be completed separately and sequentially. Once perfected, they flow together in one continuous pattern of living. Each one has an impact upon all of the others. Likewise, self-reliance is not an endpoint like the summit of a mountain, but rather a process, like the stream that flows down the mountain.

ONE FINAL MANTRA

Whether you believe in God or not, please use this spiritual formula—this mantra—to remind yourself of the message of this book:

- ''There's never been another spirit like the one within me. If I test its wisdom, I'll find Truth; heed its power, I'll have Hope; embrace its beauty, I'll know Love.''

Epilogue

It happened with Jill, Rita, Kris, and the other women who were at the Agitated or Depressed Stage of *Living Together, Feeling Alone*. First, they were hesitant to admit that they had a paradoxical death fantasy. It was a frightening thought and they tried to ignore it.

Then, after I told them that the fantasy was the desperate cry of a trapped inner child, they blurted out images that involved plane crashes, fatal falls, car accidents, cancer, and heart attacks.

Since I viewed the fantasy as only a symptom of crushing loneliness, I found little, if any, need to mention it again during our time together.

However, during our final session or at the end of a followup phone consultation, I asked each woman about her fantasy. Typically, there was a pause as if she didn't know what I was referring to. Then, with a clear note of confidence, she said, "Oh, that. It's gone. I hardly remember it."

Possibly the oddest feature of LTL is the sudden disappearance of the paradoxical death fantasy. Once a woman finds the key to her loneliness and begins a concerted effort toward self-reliance, the fantasy disappears, leaving no trace of remorse, regret, or embarrassment. (Of course, in some cases, the men *do* disappear through divorce. Even then, the fantasy disappears before he does.)

Maybe the explanation for this sudden disappearance lies in one final discovery that I made after my research was really over. True, it's a matter of emphasis, but it's an important insight nonetheless.

The woman trapped in LTL is not held captive in some remote psychological prison tower by the evil forces of loneliness. Loneliness doesn't trap her; she traps herself. Yes, she needs to find the key that opens the gate of loneliness. But she must remember that the lock is on the *inside* of the gate. It's loneliness that has to do the leaving, not the woman.

It's as if loneliness is so much thick black smoke in her soul, making it impossible for her to see and breathe. The life-threatening condition stimulates fantasies of revenge and escape. Finding the key allows the woman to open the flue on the chimney and turn on the fan. As the air clears, the smoke disappears taking the visions of death with it.

The only long-lasting mistake—if, indeed, you can call it a mistake—that the LTL woman makes is being an imperfect person who loves imperfectly. But with the key to her loneliness safely in her soul, she never again has to worry about love leading to loneliness. If it does, she knows how to release the feelings of isolation, of estrangement, and especially, of bitterness.

Each woman that I came to know during the course of my research was a study in courage. Two years ago, I would have said that each one could have moved mountains. But the traditional Indian way tells us that mountains have spirits and must be respected, not moved. So now I say that in surrendering to mountainous situations, each woman found her own inner spirituality and knew that it, too, deserved respect.

Suggested Readings

Burns, David. *Intimate Connections*. New York, NY: New American Library, 1985.

Clearly, the best popular book available on the subject of uncoupled loneliness. The self-esteem exercises are easy to understand and put into practice. This book is a great help for anyone wishing to focus on the behavioral aspects of overcoming personality shortcomings.

Jourard, Sidney. *Transparent Self: Self-Disclosure and Well-Being, 2nd ed.* New York, NY: Van Nostrand Reinhold, 1971.

I'm particularly fond of Jourard's work. He's a compassionate, yet masterful helper. "No man can come to know himself except as an outcome of disclosing himself to another person." It was with statements such as this that Jourard spawned sustained research efforts that have brought self-disclosure into the mainstream of psychological thought.

Moustakes, Clark. *Loneliness*. Englewood Cliffs, NJ: Prentice-Hall, 1961.

Although it's a bit too poetic and self-reflective at times, this remains one of the finest inspirational books I've read on loneliness. It's a perfect book to read prior to meditation. Moustakes alerted me to the possibility that the death fantasy was a cover for LTL when he said, "Aggressiveness often is a disguise of loneliness anxiety and may be expressed as cynicism and contempt for love."

Peplau, Letitia Anne and Daniel Perlman (Editors). *Loneliness: A Sourcebook of Current Theory, Research, and Therapy.* New York: John Wiley & Sons, 1982.

If you keep in mind that there are *two* types of clinical loneliness, this is an excellent resource for an in-depth study of the subject. The editors' definition of loneliness is a very important part of *Living Together, Feeling Alone*. Layperson or professional will admire and profit from this book.

Rubin, Zick. "Seeking a Cure For Loneliness." *Psychology Today.* October, 1979, pages 85–90.

It's worth a trip to the microfilm department of your local library to read Dr. Rubin's paper. He gives the reader both a social and psychological overview of loneliness, and does it in a comfortable, easy-to-read style. If you want to read just one paper on the scientific aspects of loneliness, make it this one.

Tillich, Paul. *The Eternal Now.* New York: Charles Scribner's Sons, 1963.

This is an excellent book for you to read during your solitary activity. Tillich advises you that loneliness can only be conquered by those who can master solitude. He also suggests that spiritual readings be a part of your solitude.

Weiss, Robert S. (Editor). *Loneliness: The Experience of Emotional and Social Isolation.* Cambridge: MIT Press, 1974.

Any scholarly paper on loneliness has a reference to this book. However, it's very readable by the layperson. Weiss is one of the two writers who made a passing reference to the possibility of LTL. Also, he introduced the importance of the spiritual element in loneliness with this comment: "Lonely people find themselves possessed by loneliness. No matter how hard they try to overcome it, it remains, an almost eerie affliction of their spirits."

SELF HELP

from

FAWCETT

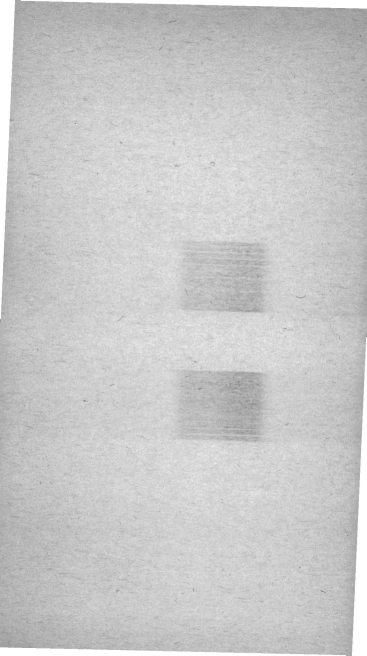